Service Process Measurement: Breaking the Code

Applying Activity Based Performance Measures to Service Processes

CAM-I
3301 Airport Freeway
Suite 324
Bedford, Texas 76021 USA
Tel: 817/860-1654
Fax: 817/275-6450
www.cam-i.org

Library of Congress
ISBN 1-890783-02-1

Service Process Measurement: Breaking the Code

Applying Activity Based Performance Measures to Service Processes

Authors:
K.J. Euske
Norm Frause
Bruce Rosenstiel
Tom Peck
Steve Schreck

Contributors:
Ray Banas
Valerie Johnston
Hugh Kemper
Theodore Kanigowski
Adrienne Tackett

Reviewers:
Debbie Frey
Jonathan Lawrence
Sandra Stirling

The CAM-I Service Process Interest Group
August 1998

CONTENTS

INTRODUCTION

This book provides a comprehensive and systematic approach to developing and applying activity-based performance measurements to processes that provide services — i.e., activities that usually have intangible outputs — within organizations. For our purposes, a process is defined as a path through a set of activities. (Fitzgerald, 1997) In manufacturing organizations, service processes primarily support and facilitate designing, producing, and delivering tangible outputs to customers. In service organizations, service processes are comprised of support as well as operational processes.

While there is extensive literature on analyzing operational processes within manufacturing organizations, there is little analysis available of service processes in either manufacturing or service organizations. This book is intended to remedy that gap and to help seasoned process managers further enhance their organization's efficacy and efficiency by extending the application of activity-based management and performance measurements to service processes.[1]

Identifying support and operational processes is a critical step towards recognizing and understanding performance improvement opportunities, however, it is not enough. Within some support processes there are activities that are directly involved in operational processes. This book will teach you to identify activities within support processes that are linked to operational processes and to measure the performance of these activities. This will allow you to trace the costs of these service activities to operational processes and give you a much clearer understanding of ways to enhance your organization's performance.

The book is organized, as shown in Figure 1, to lead the reader from the identification and analysis of the service process and related activities to the development of performance measures and an understanding of cost relationships. The next section introduces the Process Relationship Map. The map is an important tool for

[1] This guidebook does not provide an in-depth discussion of organizational behavior and change management issues. For process managers specifically interested in these subjects as they relate to service processes, an excellent reference is Heskett et al. (1997).

identifying processes and related activities as either support or operational. Once this distinction is understood, a process analysis can be executed. The Process Measurement Matrix (PMM) is then used to develop appropriate performance measures. This book concludes with three case studies that illustrate the usefulness of this approach and these tools for enhancing the performance of an organization's service processes.

Figure 1: The Organization

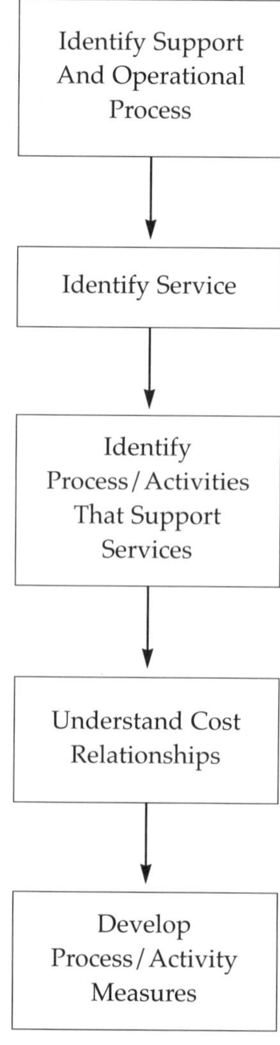

SECTION 1

Process Relationship

The Process Relationship Map leverages the Process Classification Framework, depicted in Figure 2, to ensure that all of an organization's processes and related activities are classified correctly as either support or operational. The Process Classification Framework was developed by Arthur Andersen & Co., working in close partnership with The International Benchmarking Clearing House and with the assistance of several major international corporations. The stated intent of the Process Classification Framework designers was to create a high-level, generic model to help organizations understand the relationship among operating or support processes. The designers sought to define the work performed within an organization as a set of processes and activities identified as either operational or management and support. (Arthur Andersen, 1993) Operating processes include:

- Understand markets and customers,
- Develop vision and strategy,
- Design products and services,
- Market and sell,

- Produce and deliver, and
- Invoice and service customers.

Management and support processes include:

- Develop and manage human resources,
- Manage information,
- Manage financial and physical resources,
- Execute environmental management programs,
- Manage external relationships, and
- Manage improvement and change.

By defining the work performed within an organization as consisting of either operating or support processes, and by identifying the activities they encompass, the Process Classification Framework advanced the understanding of the relationships among important and diverse processes. The Framework, however, does not address the linkage of support processes and/or relate activities to operational processes. Such linkages, when they exist, need to be identified and their costs traced for an organization to develop a clear, comprehensive understanding of their product and service costs and of opportunities to enhance the performance of both operational and support processes. To facilitate identifying these linkages, the Process Relationship Map recasts the operational and support processes into a circular model. (See Figure 3)

Figure 2: Process Classification Framework

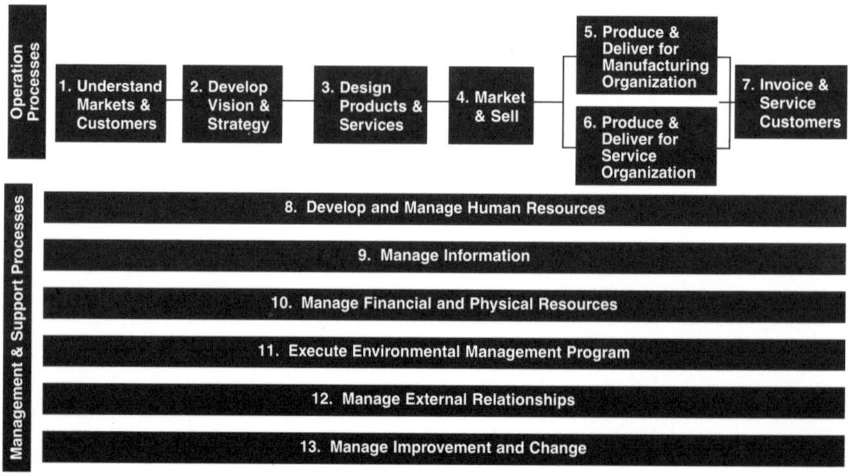

Source: Arthur Andersen, 1993

Figure 3: Process Relationship Map

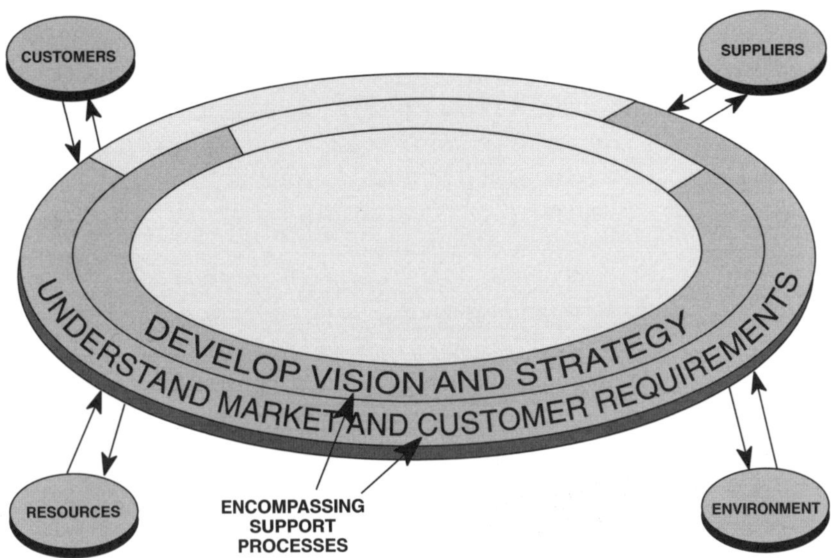

Dark Area = Traceable Costs to Operational Processes
Light Area = Non-Traceable Costs to Operational Processes

As depicted in Figure 3, the initial distinction the Process Relationship Map makes among the previously mentioned operational processes is to reclassify two of them — i.e., Understanding Market and Customer Requirements and Develop Vision and Strategy — as Encompassing Support Processes. These processes form the outside ring of the Process Relationship Map reflecting their determining influence on all other processes and related activities. Neither process, however, should be viewed as a buffer or barrier to interaction between other support and operational processes with outside constituents (e.g., customers, suppliers).

While these two processes help an organization formulate its overall strategic direction, lower-level activities within them may be traced to operational processes; there may be an identifiable causal relationship between them and one or more operational processes' product or service outputs. For example, activities within the process of Understanding Market and Customer Requirements include determining customer needs and wants, as well as monitoring changes in market or customer expectations. For a restaurant, determining customer needs and wants can be traced to an operational process as there is a direct causal relationship between it and determining specific menu items. However, monitoring changes in customer life styles, while providing guidance for the type of menu a restaurant might offer, is not a directly traceable activity. To reflect this distinction, the dark portion of the circle addresses traceable activities (i.e., the distinct steps in output generation that directly add value, sometimes called the value chain), while the light portion depicts activities that are not traceable.

Figure 4: Process Relationship Map

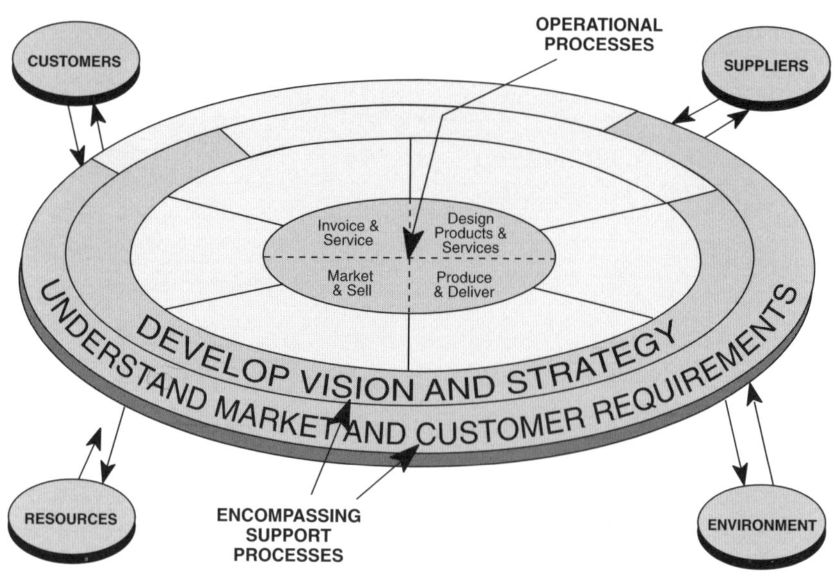

The second view of the Process Relationship Map in Figure 4 adds the operational processes that produce an organization's products and services, the value the organization creates for its customers and stakeholders. Operational processes are usually better understood and documented than support processes, and their output is directly associated with customer deliverables.

There could be activities that are actually operational within traditional support functions. In a restaurant, for example, purchasing ingredients, which is generally viewed as a support function, should

Figure 5: Process Relationship Map

Dark Area = Traceable Costs to Operational Processes
Light Area = Non-Traceable Costs to Operational Processes

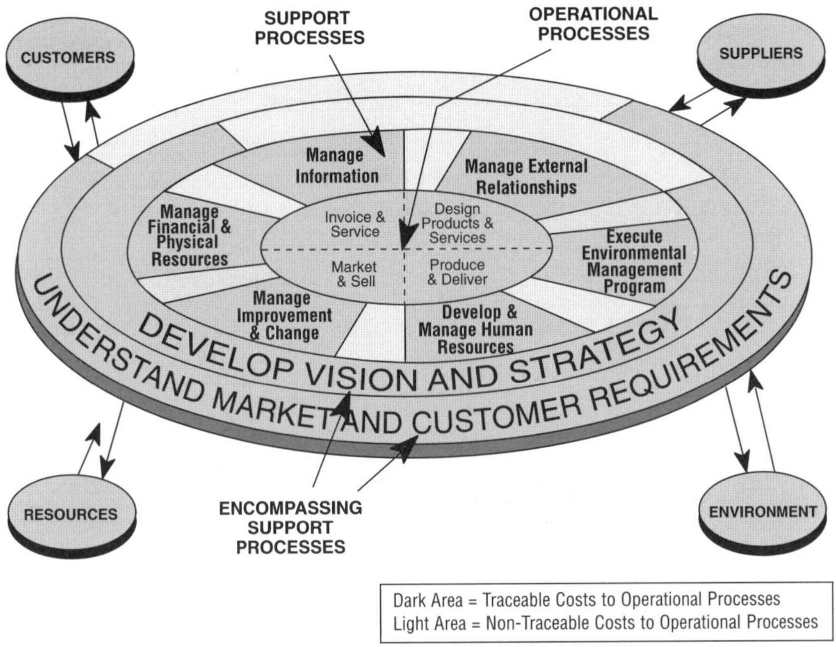

be classified as an operational activity, as it is directly linked to delivering menu selections to customers.

The complete view of the Process Relationship Map, Figure 5, incorporates the support processes, which normally include activities associated with overhead functions such as finance, facilities, and human resources. Costs of these processes are generally allocated rather than traced to operational processes. Allocations are normally based on indirect relationships, such as headcount or square footage, while tracing is based on time spent, product produced, service provided, or other more direct relationships. In order to minimize cost distortions created by allocations, it is essential to look within the support processes for activities that are traceable to operational processes.

Although Figure 5 depicts specific support processes in contact with specific operating processes (e.g. "manage information" with "invoice and service"), the support process could be traceable to each of the four operational processes. That is, "manage information" could be traceable to not only "invoice and service," but also to "market and sell," "produce and deliver," and "design products and services."

Reclassifying processes traditionally viewed as operational as support processes, and classifying support activities as operational are important concepts for enhancing an organization's understanding of its cost structure and for identifying opportunities for improving performance. Identifying all activity costs within support processes (which are directly linked with and thus traceable to operational processes) will minimize the cost distortions often associated with overhead-related allocation methods. This should be of particular interest to organizations whose accounting systems gather costs by function rather than by process. Returning to the restaurant example, the amount of time and effort required in purchasing ingredients could vary significantly by menu item. If purchasing ingredients is inappropriately classified and allocated as administrative overhead rather than as a linked operational activity, the restaurant will not have an accurate understanding of the costs of specific menu items.

In providing a framework to facilitate classifying processes and related activities, the Process Relationship Map is a valuable cost-management tool. While determining whether processes are operational or support and, whether activities within support processes are actually operational activities is not always easy, the undertaking is worth the effort. The result is a clearer understanding of the actual costs associated with an organization's products and services as well as functions. Once all processes and related activities are classified correctly, a process analysis can be performed.

SECTION 2

Process Analysis

Process analysis is a tool that traces resource consumption (e.g., labor, machine, and materials) to activities or steps within a cross-functional process. Process analysis also establishes a foundation to augment cost measures with time and quality measures to provide a more comprehensive view of process performance. Understanding the interaction among these measures provides a higher level of process knowledge to facilitate process improvement and better decision making.

Before a process analysis project is started, necessary conditions must be met to enable successful completion (CAM-I, 1997):

1. Senior management commitment to becoming a process-managed organization
2. Identifying a service or process for improvement
3. Owner of the service or process appointed and supported by senior management
4. Formation of a process analysis team with representation from all functional organizations within the process boundaries

5. Communication among, engagement of, and training of the people in the process to develop an agreement on activity definitions and process boundaries.

Only after these conditions are met, should the actual process analysis be initiated.

It is arguably more difficult to apply activity-based management concepts such as process analysis within the service or "white collar" environment, which has intangible outputs, than in the manufacturing environment. In a manufacturing environment, the processes and the component activities are typically repeated frequently, in the same manner, using a prescribed amount of resources within well-prescribed bounds to produce a tangible output. Such processes are likely to be documented relatively well.

In a service environment — such as serving a dinner in a restaurant — the process may not possess all of these characteristics. The activities associated with serving a dinner may vary from table to table and person to person at a given table. Providing service to two individuals ordering the same items may also differ and use different quantities of resources. What is encompassed in the definition of "good service" is likely to be ambiguous. However, the boundaries of the process must be specified before the activities can be defined. Identifying the specific activities must be done within the process boundaries. If we are to apply activity-based management tools and methods for effectively managing service processes, we must clearly define the boundaries and activities that form the cross-functional value chain associated with the service we are trying to manage.

The questions and answers in Table 1, filled out here with a typical company's responses, show some of the differences between dealing with a service process and a manufacturing process. The first question focuses on defining the process and its elements. The second question addresses the use of the information. The third question is concerned with developing a working understanding of the process. As the answers indicate, working with a service process will likely require more effort to develop fundamental data than is necessary for a manufacturing process.

Table 1: Service Structure Questions

QUESTION	Answers For A Service Process	Answers For A Manufacturing Process
1. Is the process defined sufficiently to communicate boundaries, inputs, outputs, customers, and suppliers?	Since services may be taken for granted or not be readily apparent, they have not been defined. Significant attention to defining services may not have been a priority. Definitions may need to be created.	Analyses of manufacturing processes have called for definitions to be created so that responsibilities are known.
2. How will process information support your ability to make effective decisions in managing your process?	The different ways that the services are performed may not be known. The provider may not understand how they want to manage the process. What seems to be a single service may require multiple processes. A restaurant may have different processes for washing pots and pans versus dishes. A mover may use different processes for moving and re-connecting computers versus desks.	Different methods of producing the output are known. Management already knows how decisions affect resource allocations.
3. Do you understand the Process?	The activities have not been identified because the service has not been defined as stated above.	The activities are identified and documented.

There are a number of process analysis models (e.g., the CAM-I Process Management Interest Group, 1997). The columns in Figure 6 depict the major elements found in most process models: suppliers, inputs, process steps, outputs and customers. Our goal in using a process model is to demonstrate how process analysis leads to the practical application of activity-based management techniques within the service processes. To this end, we focus on those parts of process analysis that provide a special challenge when considering service processes.

Figure 6: Service Process Interest Group Analysis Model

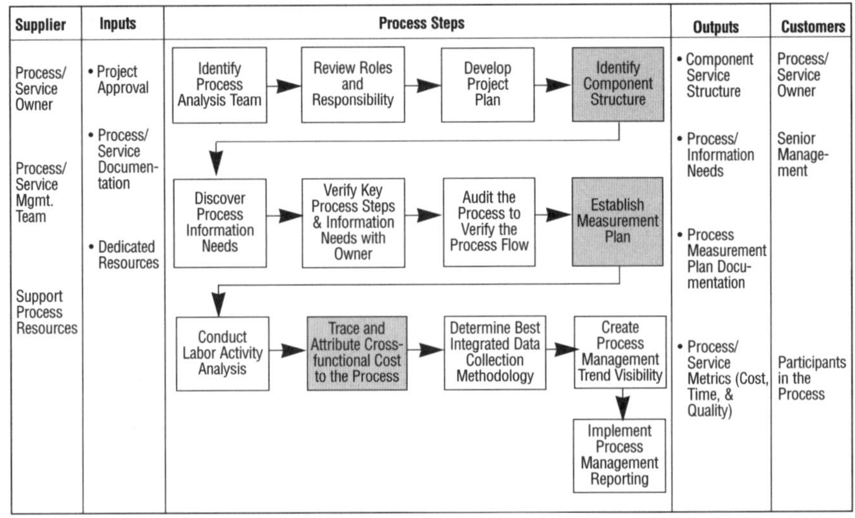

Three steps in the process analysis model in Figure 6 require special attention for analyzing services: Identify Component Structure, Establish Measurement Plan, and Trace and Attribute Cross-Functional Cost to the Process. Regardless of the process analysis model that is used, these issues will need to be addressed. In the following sections, we discuss the difficulties associated with each of these three steps and illustrate methods to deal with them.

Using the model is an iterative process. For instance, one needs to identify a process before initiating process analysis and identifying the process analysis team. Also, to Identify Component Structure involves analyzing the selected service to identify the processes and activities within that service. Doing so may mean identifying new team members, redefining roles, and creating a revised plan (reworking what you did during the previous steps in the process analysis).

IDENTIFYING COMPONENT STRUCTURE

The first step requiring special attention is Identify Component Structure. The difficulty with this step is defining the output of the service in terms of the customer and balancing that perspective with how to manage the service within the enterprise. For example, Acxiom Corporation viewed itself as a database management and network service provider. From Acxiom's perspective, it provided data lines, application software, CPU time, and database management

Figure 7: Component Structure Triangle

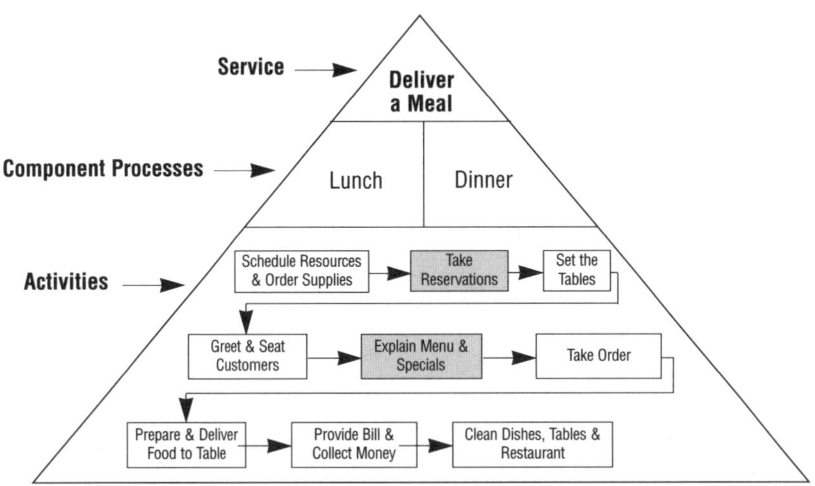

{ Shaded activities are part of the dinner process and not the lunch process }

for Automatic Teller Machines (ATMs). From the customer's perspective, Acxiom provided ATM transactions, and the customer wanted to track improvements and be billed based on these transactions. To meet customer expectations, Acxiom had to redefine its output and component process structure to report ATM transactions. Although the provider must manage the service process activities to maintain quality and customer satisfaction, the customer may not be interested in the provider's process of delivering the service.[2]

Using a restaurant example, Figure 7 portrays the relationships among a service, its component processes, and activities. The top section of the triangle represents the service delivered by the supplier, as defined from the customer's perspective. The service could be provided to other organizations or represent a support process within the organization. As in the Acxiom example, the service can be viewed from at least two perspectives. From the customer's perspective, a service represents the benefits received. The customer in a restaurant eats a meal and enjoys it. From the provider's perspective, a service

---

[2] This example is taken from the information gathered during the Activity-Based Management Best Practice Study conducted by the American Productivity and Quality Center, March 30, 1995.

includes all the processes and activities necessary to deliver those benefits.

The middle section of the triangle represents the component processes that management identified as necessary to meet the customers' needs. How the organization interprets the customers' needs should influence the management and structure of the processes. If the restaurant manages meal delivery using the distinction of lunch and dinner, management is concerned with the activities that make up those processes. If the restaurant does not alter what is provided to the customer (e.g., level of attention, menu selection at mid-day or in the evening) serving lunch and dinner would be one process, not two. Thus, the same set of activities would be applicable. Making the distinction of serving lunch and dinner implies a difference in what is expected by or delivered to the customer.

The bottom section of the triangle contains the activities that comprise component processes, which are the task-oriented flows of what is done to produce the process outputs. In Figure 7, the lunch process includes a number of activities such as: scheduling resources and ordering supplies, setting the tables, greeting and seating customers, taking orders, preparing and delivering food to tables, providing bills and collecting money, and washing dishes and cleaning tables. The dinner process includes additional activities that add complexity such as taking reservations and explaining the menu and specials.

Taken together, the activities for the restaurant in Figure 7 are the operational processes: market and sell, produce and deliver, and invoice and service. Table 2 shows the relationship between the activities in Figure 7 and the process classifications depicted in the Process Relationship Map. Note that what may have been seen as a support process, Manage Financial and Physical Resources, has been reclassified as an operational process.

In Figure 7, we focused on the service of Delivering a Meal. We could move items up or down in the hierarchy as needed. For example, we could move lunch to the top of the triangle and make the component processes cooking lunch and servicing lunch. This would bring a greater level of detail to the lower level of activities. This is useful if you decide to put more emphasis on details or find that your process improvement project is too large in scope. Moving in the other direction, you could also move Deliver a Meal down to a component process and make the service "running a restaurant." This shows the "bigger picture." It also provides less detail, making your project larger in scope. In attempting to focus in on your process, narrowing or expanding the focus of your project using this method can be beneficial.

ESTABLISHING A MEASUREMENT PLAN

The second step requiring special attention is Establishing the Measurement Plan. This step involves developing financial and non-financial measures for the service and its component processes. The difficulty with this step for a service process is defining what measurement data are necessary for managing the service. The very nature of service processes creates difficulties in defining the data. Certainly, measurements of the food's characteristics are appropriate such as quantity, quality, and appearance. However, the patron's

Table 2: Relationship of Process Classification to Component Structure

Market and Sell	Take Reservations Explain Menus and Specials Greet and Seat Customers Take Order
Produce and Deliver	Purchase Supplies Set the Table Prepare and Deliver Food to Table Clean Dishes, Table and Restaurant Schedule Resources and Order Supplies
Invoice and Service	Provide Bill and Collect Money
Manage Financial and Physical Resources	

experience will be influenced by other factors including the behavior of restaurant personnel and other patrons. Even if we could decide on a set of measures for managing serving lunch, we would likely find it difficult to collect the data. The purpose of this section is to provide a set of tools that will allow you to identify the data needed and how to collect it.

Segregation Qualities

The qualities and characteristics of a service process determine how difficult it is to define, document, and measure. These qualities and characteristics may make a service process appear to be either not well structured and difficult to analyze or well structured and more amenable to analysis. Fitzgerald et al. (1991) describe these qualities and characteristics. Fitzgerald et al. (1991) also provide a method to evaluate processes at the organizational level.

Fitzgerald et al. (1991) identified four characteristics that can be used to define service processes: intangibility, heterogeneity, simultaneity, and perishability. Intangibility is discussed in both process and output terms. For instance, the output of the service provided within a restaurant and the overall dining experience is considered intangible. However, the food and its preparation is more tangible; the input is measurable and known and the process is repetitive. The relative intangibility of a process and its output can be identified by answering questions such as the following: Is there a tangible product, capable of being consistently duplicated and delivered at the end of a systematic repetitive process? Alternatively, is the successful outcome dependent on a combination of some output and customized support (e.g., the well-presented meal served by a knowledgeable and helpful server)? Can quality be measured through statistical process control? Is value likely to be defined differently from one diner to the next?

Heterogeneity is driven by a high labor component within the process. Hibachi chefs, therapists, seminar leaders, circus clowns, or consultants may perform their respective processes multiple times, but the outcomes will differ from occurrence to occurrence and from provider to provider. It is difficult to ensure consistent performance from the same individual, let alone to get comparability between individuals.

Simultaneity occurs when production and consumption coincide.

Getting a physical exam, renting a hotel room, and having a massage are examples of simultaneous processes.

Perishability describes a service that cannot be stored; the product is consumed immediately. Haircuts, massages, physical exams, hotel rooms, and restaurant and theater seats cannot be stockpiled and sold later. Once the event or time has passed, the opportunity for a sale is gone forever.

Each service process is more or less intangible, heterogeneous, simultaneous, and perishable. The position of the process within that spectrum affects the performance measurement system, "not so much in terms of what is measured, but how it is measured." (Fitzgerald et al., 1991, p. 3) Simultaneous processes are normally perishable. Heterogeneous, simultaneous, perishable processes are quite often intangible. Equipment-focused processes, which will be covered in more detail in the following section, are normally more homogeneous and not as simultaneous as people-focused processes.

SERVICE TYPES AND CLASSIFICATION DIMENSIONS

Fitzgerald et al. (1991) define "three different generic service types: professional services, service shops, and mass services" (1991, p. 9) that are representative of all service businesses. "Professional services are defined as high-contact organizations where customers spend a considerable time in the service process." (Fitzgerald et al., 1991, p. 9) The processes are people and front-office focused, with process performance emphasized over product, and the tasks are heterogeneous in nature. Consulting firms are representative of this service type.

"Service shops are characterized by levels of customer contact, customization, volumes of customers and staff discretion which position them between the extremes of professional and mass services." (Fitzgerald et al., 1991, p. 13) Most wholesale, retail shops, and restaurants will fit this category.

"Mass services have many customer transactions, involving limited contact time and little customization. The processes are equipment based and product oriented, with most value added in the back office and little judgment applied by the front office staff." (Fitzgerald et al., 1991, p. 11) Railroads, airlines, and hotels are all indicative of mass service.

Each service type is "differentiated in terms of the volume of customers processed by a typical unit per day against six other classification dimensions:

- people/equipment focus
- front/back office focus
- product/process focus
- level of customization of the service to any one customer
- discretion available to front office staff
- contact time available by front office staff" (Fitzgerald et al., p. 9)

When completed, Table 3, the CAM-I Service Classification Grid, graphically depicts this spectrum. The two outside columns contain the classification characteristics. The three center columns are the service types, from mass services to professional services.
The relative ease of cost traceability distinguishes each service type. Professional services are the easiest to trace, due to the people-based processes directed towards specific customers. Mass services are most difficult due to the high use of equipment (i.e., capital directed towards many customers simultaneously). Service shops need to be examined on a case-by-case basis depending on where they fall within the continuum. The service-type classification scheme allows businesses within different industries to recognize a commonality of issues, problems, and processes, enabling similar measures to be used and external benchmarking to occur.

Table 3: CAM-I Service Classification Grid

Classification Dimension	Mass Service	Service Shop	Professional Service	Classification Dimension
Equipment focus				People focus
Back-office focus				Front-office focus
Product focus				Process focus
Low level of customization of the service to any one customer				High level of customization of the service to any one customer
Minimal discretion available to front office staff				Considerable discretion available to front office staff
Minimal contact time available by front office staff				Considerable contact time available by front office staff

APPLYING THE CLASSIFICATION DIMENSIONS

By viewing each process as an independent entity from an internal or external customer's perspective, we can determine which service type (i.e., professional service, service shop, mass service) the process most closely resembles. The six classification dimensions listed in Table 3 are the attributes used to distinguish the processes by service type. The answers to the classification dimensions questions in Table 4 enable us to classify the process by service type. These questions can be applied to any process or activity.

Applying these questions to our restaurant example, we find that the process depends both on people and equipment; the restaurant staff is important in the process but the food preparation equipment and the furnishings in the dining area are also important. The value received by the customer is dependent on both the interaction with the restaurant staff in the dining area (front office), and the actual meal served from the kitchen (back office).

The customer does receive a tangible product, but the process of delivering it is also important. The manner in which the service is delivered to each customer is quite similar. The restaurant personnel do not have a great deal of latitude to make decisions affecting the meal that will be served. Finally, the staff spends a considerable amount of time in contact with the customer.

Table 4: Classification Dimension Questions

1) Is the process dependent on people or equipment?
2) Is the value the customer receives dependent on the interaction with the organization's representatives or the organization's product?
3) Is the value received from a tangible product or does the customer participate in a service process?
4) Is each iteration, sale, or event unique or customized to the customer?
5) How much latitude does the personnel interacting with the customer have?
6) How much time does the interacting personnel have with the customer?

If we answered these same questions for a fast-food franchise of a large chain, we would get some different answers. For example, the fast food franchise is much more equipment focused. There is strong product focus. Each sale has less variation than in the restaurant. There is minimal "eating area" staff. The staff has virtually no latitude to make decisions regarding what will be served. A minimal amount of time is spent by the staff dealing with the customer.

Table 5 shows the classifications that resulted from analyzing these two organizations. The completed grid presents a profile of the two services. The results for the restaurant indicate that it primarily has the characteristics of a service shop with some characteristics of both mass and professional services. The fast-food franchise is primarily a mass service with some characteristics of a service shop. The identifying characteristics will help us determine what to measure, both from the customer's perspective and from the organization's.

Table 5: Classification of the Restaurant and Fast-Food Franchise

Classification Dimension	Mass Service	Service Shop	Professional Service	Classification Dimension
Equipment focus		♦ ●		People focus
Back-office focus	♦	●		Front-office focus
Product focus	♦	●		Process focus
Low level of customization of the service to any one customer	♦ ●			High level of customization of the service to any one customer
Minimal discretion available to front office staff	♦	●		Considerable discretion available to front office staff
Minimal contact time available by front office staff	♦		●	Considerable contact time available by front office staff

Restaurant ●
Fast-Food Franchise ♦

DIMENSIONS OF PERFORMANCE

The work of Fitzgerald et al. (1991) provides a foundation for us to develop a measurement system that links the levels in the Component Structure Triangle (Figure 7, pg. 13). The goal is to create a set of measures that link activities to the service process.

Fitzgerald, et al. (1991) identified six dimensions of performance that are applicable to all three service types:

1. Competitiveness
2. Financial performance
3. Quality of service
4. Flexibility
5. Resource utilization
6. Innovation

They argue that the dimensions are critical at the organization level, because used in combination, the dimensions provide a balanced view of the organization. Each of these dimensions will have greater or lesser emphasis, depending on the organization's strategy and environment. Examples of the dimensions and measures are presented in Table 6.

Table 6: Dimensions of Performance and Types of Measures

	DIMENSIONS OF PERFORMANCE	TYPES OF MEASURES
RESULTS	Competitiveness	Relative market share and position Sales growth Measure of the customer base
	Financial performance	Profitability Liquidity Capital Structure Market Ratios
DETERMINANTS	Quality of service	Reliability Responsiveness Aesthetics/appearance Cleanliness/tidiness Comfort Friendliness Communication Courtesy Competence Access Availability Security
	Flexibility	Volume flexibility Delivery speed flexibility Specification flexibility
	Resource utilization	Productivity Efficiency
	Innovation	Performance of the innovation process Performance of individual innovations

Source: Fitzgerald et al., 1991, p. 8

DEVELOPING THE MEASUREMENT SYSTEM

For an organization to be successful in developing its measurement system, it must start with a clear statement of its unique competencies, a clear understanding of what its market and customers value, and have a strategic vision to achieve its goals. The manner in which it will offer its services (i.e., the service type it chooses) must then be determined to ensure support of its strategy and vision within its operating environment.

Only after the organization-level measures are defined and the service type is determined can each process owner or team identify process-level performance dimensions, measures, and performance targets that link to the organization level. The process-level dimensions and measures should be based on the output and processes described during identification of the component structure, at the early stages of the process analysis.

Once the process measurement system is developed, performance dimensions, measures, and performance targets that are linked to the processes can be developed for process performers and process owners. Process-performer and owner measures can provide incentives for specific behaviors that will result in positive process performance. The selected process dimensions, measures, and performance targets should minimize conflict for the process performer.

For example, the goal of the fast food establishment is to "quickly serve food of consistent quality, at a reasonable price." The goal of the restaurant is to "provide fresh meals at affordable prices in a pleasing environment." At the process level, the management of both organizations wants efficiency to be a measure of resource utilization, and customer satisfaction to be an indicator of quality for the meal delivery process. How process performers should balance the two potentially conflicting measures must be addressed in the design stage. In a fast-food setting, fast service may equate to customer satisfaction. For a meal in the restaurant, having all courses served at the same time may negatively affect customer satisfaction. Care must be taken to develop performance measures for the process performers that support both efficiency and customer satisfaction targets.

In another industry, the vision of an organization might be the "easiest organization to do business with." Focus groups defined "easiest organization to do business with" as customers having a single point of contact for all questions, queries, and orders with the organization. To achieve this vision, the Provide After-Sales Service, Respond to Customer Inquiries, and Process Customer Orders processes will need to be handled by the same knowledgeable customer representative. The measure of achieving the vision will be the responses to specific questions on customer satisfaction surveys. However, satisfying the customer at any cost is usually not a viable strategy. Therefore, measures that complement and balance customer satisfaction must be selected.

Two such balancing measures are employee satisfaction and cost effectiveness. Employee satisfaction can be measured by resources allocated to employee development and results of employee satisfaction surveys. Cost effectiveness can be measured by cost per unit, cycle time, and number of customer representatives per a certain number of customers. Additionally, employee satisfaction not only balances customer satisfaction measurements, but it may also serve as a leading indicator for customer satisfaction.

The discussion in this section, thus far, has been an overview of developing the measurement system. The balance of this section focuses on a framework for developing process measures.

THE SERVICE PROCESS MEASUREMENT MATRIX

Selecting appropriate process measures can be difficult due to any number of factors, such as the process complexity, the number of possible items to measure, the difficulty in gathering the information, or the state of the segregation qualities (i.e., intangibility, heterogeneity, simultaneity, and perishability) within the process. By using the CAM-I Process Measurement Matrix (PMM) (Table 7), we can organize a company's measurement scheme to support vertically integrated financial and non-financial aspects of performance. The PMM brings together the Arthur Andersen/International Benchmarking Clearinghouse Process Classification Framework and Fitzgerald et al.'s (1991) organization-level service types and measurements to create a framework for measurement identification and linkage, as well as potential cost tracing at the process level. In a later section we use the matrix to document representative measurement system and demonstrate its balance and breadth.

Each process, sub-process, and activity from the Arthur Andersen/International Benchmarking Clearinghouse Process Classification Framework is listed in the far left column of the PMM in Table 7. In the first column, the Produce and Deliver Meals Process is listed with its support processes and activities. Fitzgerald et al's (1991) service types — professional services, service shops, and mass services — head the next three columns. The dimensions of performance — financial performance, quality, flexibility, and resource utilization — follow in the last four columns. Two of the performance dimensions were not included: competitiveness and innovation. The PMM does not include the competitiveness dimension because it is fundamentally a measure of how successful an organization is in the marketplace and is not relevant to the process level. Innovation is excluded because innovation success is reflected by improvement/ deterioration within the other performance dimensions (see Fitzgerald et al., 1991, p. 106). Financial performance was included (although it is similar to innovation in that it is a resultant or lagging measure) because of the importance of understanding cost at a process and activity level. The other three dimensions (quality, flexibility, and resource utilization) are determinant or leading measures that provide information that is critical to the customer or process manager.

Identifying the performance dimensions that are important for the major or high-level processes is the initial step in completing the PMM. What the organization's markets and customers value and its strategic vision should provide the criteria to identify the dimensions. After the high-level measures are defined, successive layers of the process are reviewed to determine if the performance dimensions are necessary at that level, and if so, with the same measure or a different measure.

Table 7: CAM-I Process Measurement Matrix (PMM)

	Service Type			Dimension of Performance			
Process, Sub-process, Activity from the IBC Process Classification Framework	Mass Services	Service Shop	Professional Services	Financial Performance	Quality	Flexibility	Resource Utilization
PRODUCE AND DELIVER MEALS							
Plan for and acquire necessary resources or inputs							
Acquire capital goods (restaurant, stoves, computer)							
Hire employees							
Obtain materials and supplies (cooking, cleaning)							
Obtain appropriate technology							
Convert resources or inputs into products							
Develop and adjust production process							
Schedule production (breads, soups, food prep)							
Move materials and resources							
Make product (meals)							
Package and store the product (if appropriate)							
Stage the product for delivery (move to counter)							
Make delivery							
Arrange product shipment (delivery)							
Deliver products to customers (table service)							
Install (if specified)							
Manage produce and deliver process							
Document and monitor order status							
Manage inventories (frozen, pre-packaged, daily)							
Assure quality Schedule and perform maintenance (cleaning)							
Monitor environmental constraints (EPA, FDA)							

PROCESS MEASURES

The appropriate measures within a process are indicated by the organization's performance dimensions and measures, the type of service process, and the planned outcome of the process. The performance measures should provide management with decision-making information based on what is important to the customer and meeting the organization's goals. Within those parameters, process type and output can guide the measurement process. For a people-focused, highly-customized process with varying inputs and customer specific outputs (e.g., course development, market planning), quality of service and not resource utilization would be an important performance dimension. For an equipment focused, repetitive process with known inputs and constant output (e.g., fast-food preparation and delivery), resource utilization would likely be appropriate.

A service process's position within the spectrum of the segregation qualities (intangibility, heterogeneity, simultaneity, and perishability) will indicate how to measure the selected performance attribute. When the process is homogenous with constant input, output, and process (e.g., accounts payable processing) the productivity measures may include traditional yield and efficiency measures reported through time and volume collection. When the input varies in complexity and the process includes greater human interaction (e.g., developing budgets) the measures are not likely to include yield and efficiency measures, but may be limited to measures of cycle time and resources used.

PERFORMANCE MEASUREMENT QUESTIONS

This section presents a set of questions to assist in determining specific measures. The restaurant example is used to demonstrate the application of the questions. After using the Service Classification Grid (Table 3, page 19) and the PMM (Table 7) to determine the type of process and the relevant performance dimensions for the high-level process (in this case, "produce and deliver meals"), we can begin to determine the appropriate process-level performance measures by answering the questions in Table 8. These questions were selected after evaluating the critical factors identified in several texts (e.g., Chang and De Young, 1995; Fitzgerald et al., 1991; Hronec, 1993; Kaplan, 1992).

The answers to the questions in Table 8 will form the basis for your measures. The selected measures should have a customer focus, be cost effective to implement and be vertically integrated. Answering the questions will identify obsolete measures that can be retired leaving the new measures focused on the "right" data. The transition to a customer orientation may spur the retirement of traditional productivity measures in favor of customer-satisfaction and problem-resolution measures.

As an example, using the Arthur Anderson/International Benchmarking Clearing House Process Classification Framework we select the sub-process "convert resources or inputs into products" to represent the conversion of raw ingredients into meals. To develop measures for the restaurant's sub-process, we will first need to understand, and develop, the organization and process-level measures.

Organization Level. For our restaurant, the answers to the organizational-level measurement questions are:

- What is the vision/mission of the organization?
  To provide fresh meals at affordable prices in a pleasing environment.
- What is the organization's unique competency?
  Affordability in an upscale atmosphere.

The answers to the next three questions are presented in Table 9. The first column of Table 9 displays the performance dimensions at the organizational level. Although competitiveness is one of the dimensions at the organizational level, with associated measures and targets, it is not a dimension that is directly applicable at the process level. The second column contains the dimensions' attributes. The last two columns are the actual measures and the associated targets.

Table 8: Performance Measurement Questions

Organization Level - data to gather rather than questions to answer

- What is the vision / mission of the organization?
- What is the organization's unique competency?
- What are the organization-level dimensions of performance?
- What are the organization-level measures?
- What are the organization-level performance targets?

Process Level

Linked to Organization (Not all are necessarily linked/related to your processes)

- How do my processes support/relate to the organization-level dimensions of performance?
- How do my processes support/relate to the organization-level measures?
- How can I measure the aspects of my process that relate to the organization-level dimensions of performance and measures? (The answer is partially dependent on the service-type and segregation qualities.)

Customer Focused

- What do my customers value?
- How can I measure what my customers' value? (The answer is partially dependent on the service-type and segregation qualities.)

Balancing

- Do these measures provide for a balanced view of my processes?
- What additional measures would provide a balanced view?
- What additional information do I need to manage the organization/process?
- Do I need to be able to support other initiatives (CPI, TQM, ABC/M, Pricing strategies, Supply Chain Management, etc.)?

Practicality

- Do I have tracking systems in place?
- Is it cost effective to develop the tracking system(s)?
- Which measures that I am already tracking meet the new requirements?
- Which measures will I retire with the implementation of the new measures?

Table 9: Restaurant Dimensions of Performance, Measures and Performance Targets at the Organizational Level

Dimension of Performance	Types of Measures	Key Measures	Performance Targets
Financial Performance	*Revenue Growth*	(Current year revenue - prior year revenue) / prior year revenue	6.5 %
Financial Performance	*Cost effectiveness*	Spoiled ingredients / Gross ingredients	5 %
Financial Performance	*Net Income*	Revenue – Expenses	$145,000
Quality of Service	*Customer* Satisfaction	Percent of repeat credit card users to total credit card users	75 %
Competitiveness	*Customer Growth*	(Number of current year customers – number of prior year customers) / prior year customers	15%
Resource Utilization	*Employee Satisfaction*	Percent of employees who respond excellent or good on the employee opinion survey	80%
Resource Utilization	*Employee Turnover*	Number of employees leaving the company / [(number of employees at the beginning of the year + the number of employees at the end of the year)/2]	25 %
Quality of Service	*Customer Complaints*	Number of complaints / number of customers	2 %

Process Level. The answers to the process-level measurement questions for linking the sub-process to the organization are:

- How do my processes support/relate to the organization-level performance dimensions?

  The Produce and Deliver process and the sub-process (Convert Resources or Inputs into Products) have both direct and indirect relationships to all of the organization level performance dimensions. Cost effectiveness is a direct result of accurately forecasting the number of meals consumed so that the proper amount of ingredients is purchased each day. Customer-growth, customer-satisfaction, and employee-satisfaction performance measures are indirectly driven by the size or quality of the meal and the level of service. The relationship between repeat business and satisfied customers is dependent on successfully performing these processes.

- How do my processes relate to or support the organization-level measures?

    The Produce and Deliver process (Manage Inventories and Obtain Materials and Supplies) will support the cost effectiveness measure. Make Product (meal) and Deliver Product (meal) influence the customer and financial measures.

- How can I measure the aspects of my process that relate to the organization-level dimensions of performance and measures? (The answer is partially dependent on the service-type and segregation qualities.)

    The sub-processes and activities within Produce and Deliver have the attributes of a service shop. The process is dependent on both people and equipment; the restaurant staff is important in the process but the food preparation equipment and the furnishings in the dining area are also important. The sub-processes have mostly tangible inputs and outputs and are repeated rather consistently. Although there is variability on a meal-by-meal, customer-by-customer, or table-by-table basis, viewed in aggregate the processes can be considered as homogeneous with tangible outputs and thus subject to quantifiable measures.

As the measures indicate problems, the sub-processes can be further decomposed and measures implemented for additional cost objects. The heterogeneity that is masked at the summary level will become apparent at more detailed levels of the process.

A rule-of-thumb is to develop initial measures at a high level, identifying the supporting sub-processes and capturing additional measures, as appropriate. When problems occur, capture additional measures to determine root causes. When the problems are resolved, discontinue reporting those measures. For instance, measuring the amount (dollars/quantity) of unused materials each day in relationship to the total amount purchased would yield an indicator of over buying and poor forecasting.

As a second example, the value received by the customer is dependent on both the interaction with the restaurant staff in the dining area (front office) and the actual meal served from the kitchen (back office). Observing customer interaction with the wait staff and observing the amount of uneaten portions may provide a leading indicator of customer satisfaction. Customer and employee survey results could also provide quantifiable indicators of opportunity areas. The answers to the customer-focused, process-level measurement questions are:

- What do the customers value?

  A customer is any user of the process: paying customers, management, and the employees. The paying customers of this restaurant value service quality along with the appearance and cleanliness of the restaurant. They also value the friendliness and courtesy of the staff and big, tasty servings. The management values resource utilization, flexibility of the produce and deliver product sub-processes, cost effectiveness of external suppliers, and consumption forecast reliability. The employees value a safe, clean, busy environment with customers that tip well.

- How can I measure what the customers value? (The answer is partially dependent on the service type and segregation qualities.)

  The characteristics of service quality that the paying customers value can be measured through surveys and observations. One way is through survey or comment cards that are available at the table or distributed with the check. A more complicated and expensive option is to develop a calling list from credit card customers. A more qualitative approach is for the manager to stop by customers' tables or for the waiter or cashier to query the clientele. Another measure could be the number and frequency of repeat customers.

  Due to the homogeneity of the processes at the sub-process level, resource utilization and flexibility can be measured through averages and gross counts such as number of meals served divided by number of hours of operation, number of meals served divided by number of employees, average time to prepare specific meals, average customer time spent at lunch or dinner, or average customer wait time. As mentioned earlier, cost effectiveness can be measured by dividing the amount (dollars/quantity) of spoiled materials each day by the total amount purchased.

Employees value characteristics similar to the customers. Their satisfaction with security, cleanliness, and customer volume can be measured through surveys or determined through employee meetings.

The answers to the measurement questions addressing balance at the process level are:

- Do the measures provide for a balanced view of my processes?

  The measures provide for a relatively balanced view of the process, since they balance customers' perception of service quality with measures of resource utilization, flexibility, and cost effectiveness. The employees' view of the characteristics they value may provide a leading indicator of potential customer problems. This is because employees may value some of the same characteristics customers do.

- What additional measures would provide a more balanced view?

  Financial performance measures can be developed to provide variable-process and meal costs. These costs can be used to develop pricing strategies for lunches, dinners, and specials.

- What additional information do I need to manage the process?

  We need to track Health Department regulations.

- Do I need to be able to support other initiatives, such as continuous process improvement (CPI), total quality management (TQM), activity-based cost management (ABC/M), pricing strategies, supply chain management?

  Management might want to support a quality supplier program and measure the performance of certified suppliers.

The answers to the measurement questions addressing practicality at the process level are:

- Are tracking systems in place?

  Yes and no. There are records of all the credit card transactions. Formal tools do not exist to report the number of repeat customers and how much they spend. Although the restaurant has comment cards, customers have not been actively encouraged to complete them.

- Is it cost effective to develop the tracking system(s)?

  Yes. It would be relatively simple to develop a simple database application to track and report repeat customers. Comment cards can be distributed with the credit card forms to encourage participation. Employees can be surveyed to ensure that suppliers are meeting standard performance levels.

- Which measures that I am already tracking meet the new requirements?

  It appears that the repeat customer measure is at least partially in place.

- Which measures will I retire with the implementation of the new measures?

  The length of time customers occupy a table is currently measured. It is not necessary information for the new measurement system.

Using the answers to the above questions, the completed matrix for the Produce and Deliver process is produced in Table 10. By reviewing the table, you can see that the measures are balanced across the major process. There are links to the sub-processes and measures across multiple dimensions in the areas critical to the external customer. It is possible to scan the sub-processes and activities to determine if additional measures will yield information for decision making.

Table 10: Completed CAM-I Process Measurement Matrix

	Service Type			Dimension of Performance			
Process, Sub-process, Activity from the IBC Process Classification Framework	Mass Services	Service Shop	Professional Services	Financial Performance	Quality	Flexibility	Resource Utilization
PRODUCE AND DELIVER MEALS		•		*	*	*	*
Plan for and acquire necessary resources or inputs			•				
Acquire capital goods (restaurant, stoves, computer)							
Hire employees							
Obtain materials and supplies (cooking, cleaning)					*		
Obtain appropriate technology							
Convert resources or inputs into products		•			*	*	*
Develop and adjust production process							
Schedule production (breads, soups, food prep)							
Move materials and resources							
Make product (meals)					*	*	
Package and store the product (if appropriate)							
Stage the product for delivery (move to counter)							
Make delivery			•		*		
Arrange product shipment (delivery)							
Deliver products to customers (table service)					*	*	
Install (if specified)							
Manage produce and deliver process		•					
Document and monitor order status							
Manage inventories (frozen, pre-packaged, daily)							
Assure quality Schedule and perform maintenance (cleaning)							
Monitor environmental constraints (EPA, FDA)							

• Service Type
* Dimension of Performance

SECTION 3

Trace and Attribute Cross-Functional Costs to the Process

The third step that requires special attention is tracing and attributing cross-functional costs to the process. Traceability refers to the relative ease with which a cost is traced to an outcome or cost object. Traceable costs are those which can be assigned to cost objects through appropriate resource drivers. Non-traceable costs are allocated or managed as a pool. Some financial and cost management control systems do not provide the information necessary to trace cross-functional costs. These systems focus primarily on managing the budgets and actual cost of functional organizations, which are analyzed using general ledger accounts such as labor, travel, supplies, and depreciation expense. It is often difficult — if not impossible — to identify process costs using the data available. If the accounting system cannot provide the cost data, using surveys or estimates may provide the data needed for process costing.

Understanding the service and its related activities

by developing the component structure, and understanding the service type will provide guidance for tracing costs. Table 11 is a tool that provides recommendations for tracing labor and non-labor cost for each service type. Mass services, professional services, and service shops each consume labor and non-labor resources. If the service and its related activities have been defined at levels below which data are collected, an employee survey may be necessary as a preliminary step in attributing labor cost to the process. Furthermore, the measurement plan may require labor and non-labor costs by region or customer. This will drive the need to use estimation, off-the-books records, service/scheduling systems, time cards, or surveys to trace cost to the desired level.

The Identify Component Structure and Establish Measurement Plan steps can help identify what and how costs can be traced. Identifying the component structure helps by highlighting the activities needed to manage and perform the service. Knowing the activities enables the identification of the end-to-end labor and non-labor resources incorporated in the value chain.

The answers to the performance measurement questions within the Establish Measurement Plan step provide an indication of how traceable the costs are in relation to service type. For example, since professional service processes are people-based with direct labor representing a high percentage of the total costs, tracing costs, and revenues to customers and services is not extremely difficult. Professional service enterprises (e.g., attorneys and consultants) have time reporting systems in place to capture time spent per customer or project. These time reporting systems can be readily established for service processes within an organization. However, within some organizations tradition may be a barrier to implementing such systems.

Mass services and service shops, on the other hand, are more equipment-based and have processes that produce "multiple, heterogeneous and joint inseparable services through which customers may consume different mixes of services" (Fitzgerald et al., 1991, p.24) making traceability of costs more difficult.

In the restaurant example, delivering a meal has a mix of mass service and service shop characteristics. Therefore, we will probably be able to trace costs to only the service or its component processes and

Table 11: Cost Tracing Preconditions and Concerns

Service Type	Resource	Data Source	Data Source/Method
Mass	Equipment	Equipment/maintenance General ledger labor costs	Off-the-books equipment, records or estimation
	Labor	General ledger labor costs traced to the service by survey/estimation	Service/scheduling systems data used to trace labor hours to the service
	Other non-labor	General ledger non-labor costs	Off-the-books records or estimation
Service shop	Labor	Combination of on and off-the-books- labor collection systems	Survey for estimated times
	Non-labor	Combination of General Ledger non-labor costs and off-the-book estimation	
Professional Service	Labor	General Ledger labor costs timesheets	Operational labor collection records
	Non-labor	General ledger non-labor	Operational non-labor collection records

not to activities. In Figure 8, a resource such as kitchen staff can be traced to the "prepare and deliver food" and "clean dishes, table, and restaurant" activities. However, the cost of utilities is not traceable to a specific activity. The cost of utilities is captured at the level of service provided, "deliver a meal."

For all service types, traceability is enhanced by capturing time spent and resources used at the activity level. The elapsed time for the activity can be captured through either time reports or percent-of-time estimates. The information can be captured weekly, monthly, quarterly, or annually, depending on the organization's requirements. However, for joint or inseparable products, allocations may be the only method of assigning costs to the specific product.

When the activity or product cost information is necessary for decision making, tracking mechanisms should be established to

Figure 8: Process Model

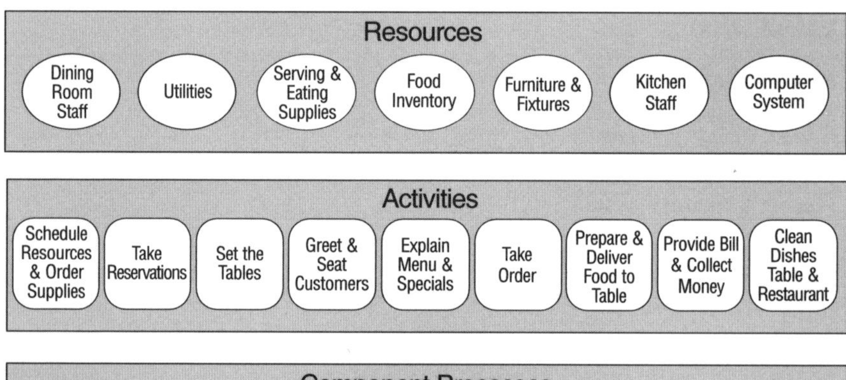

facilitate their reporting. Questions to determine the necessity and value of tracking the cost are:

1. Is the process cost-significant?
2. Is the value received by the internal or external customer substantial?
3. Is the process value-adding?
4. Is the process cost high in proportion to others?
5. Is the data-collection cost greater than the potential benefit?
6. Is the cost information critical to pricing or outsourcing decisions?

The focus is on gathering the critical or necessary information for decision-making. Cost collection should not be undertaken just for the sake of doing it.

The difficulties encountered working with service processes can be overcome through concentrated use of the Process Relationship Map (Figure 5) and Analysis Model (Figure 6). Cost, time, and quality measures for service processes can be quantified and used to generate maximum service performance.

CONCLUSION

You now have been introduced to a comprehensive and systematic approach to developing and applying activity-based performance measures to processes that provide services. Figure 9 depicts the principal elements of the approach from the identification and analysis of the service process and related activities to the development of performance measures and an understanding of cost relationships. Appendix A contains a more detailed checklist of the steps necessary to implement the approach. Appendix B contains copies of selected tables and figures from the book.

The following section contains three case studies that provide extended examples of applying the techniques developed in this book. The first case study explores process analyses conducted at The Boeing Company. The case highlights three points: the use of the process model, the use of the component structure to understand how a process is managed, and managing with a combination of financial and non-financial measures. The second case study examines the development of process measures at GTE Directories Corporation. The case features the use of the performance measurement questions. The third case study looks at how the Marine Corps, a government agency, used the service process method. The case study examines the use of both the process relationship map and the component structure triangle to help identify the critical activities within a process. The case study focuses on measuring non-financial performance such as reduced cycle time and improved quality.

Figure 9: Elements of the Service Process Analysis

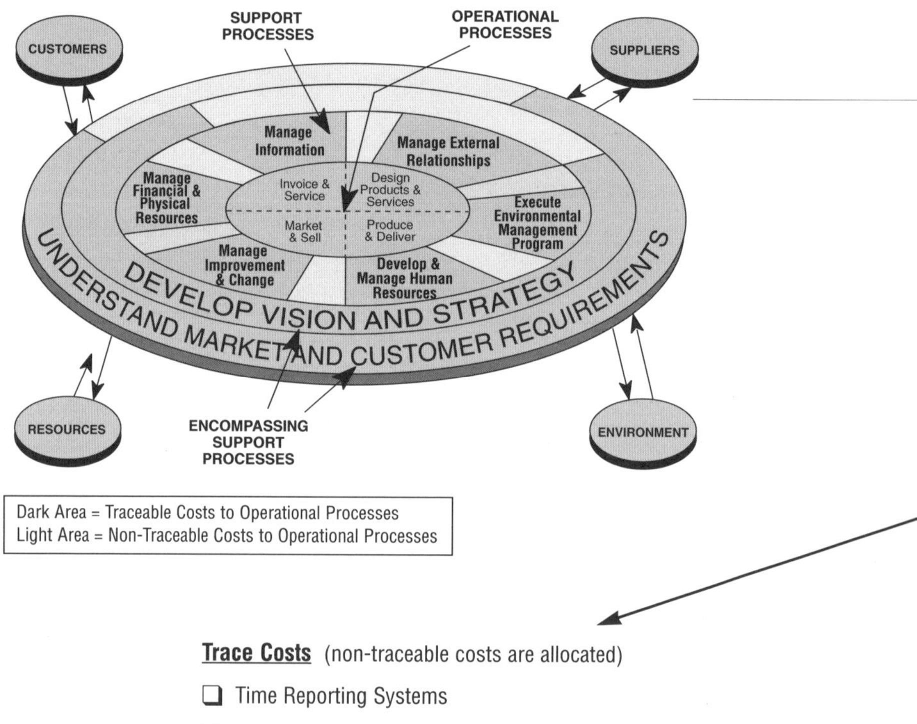

Dark Area = Traceable Costs to Operational Processes
Light Area = Non-Traceable Costs to Operational Processes

Trace Costs (non-traceable costs are allocated)

- ❑ Time Reporting Systems
- ❑ Estimation Techniques
- ❑ Financial Systems
- ❑ ABC
- ❑ Other

Classification Dimension	Mass Service	Service Shop	Professional Service	Classification Dimension
Equipment focus				People focus
Back-office focus				Front-office focus
Product focus				Process focus
Low level of customization of the service to any one customer				High level of customization of the service to any one customer
Minimal discretion available to front office staff				Considerable discretion available to front office staff
Minimal contact time available by front office staff				Considerable contact time available by front office staff

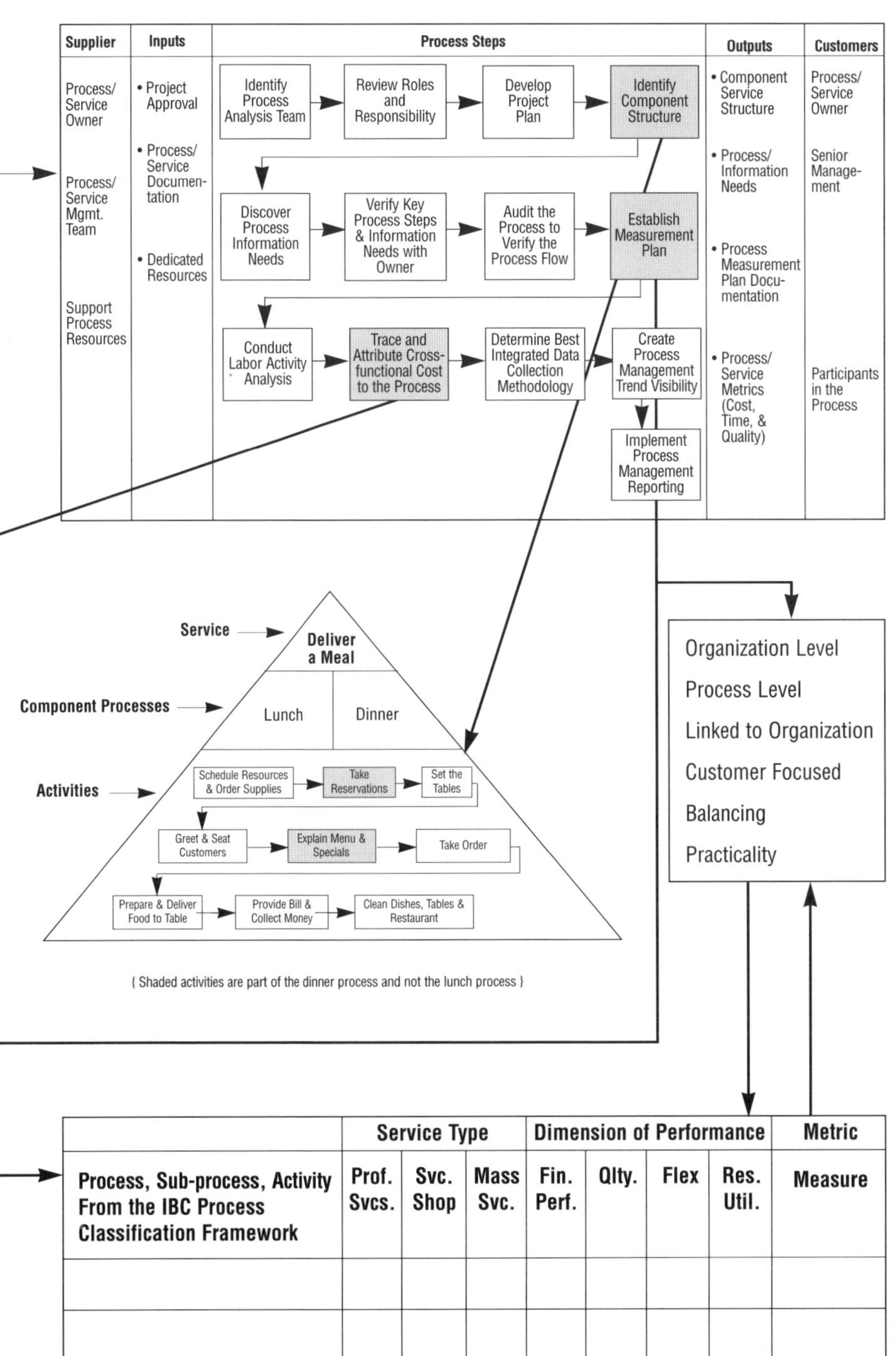

	Service Type			Dimension of Performance				Metric
Process, Sub-process, Activity From the IBC Process Classification Framework	**Prof. Svcs.**	**Svc. Shop**	**Mass Svc.**	**Fin. Perf.**	**Qlty.**	**Flex**	**Res. Util.**	**Measure**

SECTION 4

CAM-I CASE STUDY: Boeing Information and Support Services Computing Restoration Service

Steve Schreck
The Boeing Company

BACKGROUND

Beginning with the B & W seaplane in 1916, the Boeing Company has built on its presence in the aerospace industry. Today, serving as the largest aerospace company in the world, Boeing organizes itself around two operating divisions: Commercial Airplane and Information, Space & Defense Systems.

To best support the shared services needs of its operating divisions, the Information & Support Services (ISS) division was formed. Currently organized as part of the Shared Services Group, ISS provides computing, administrative, safety, environmental, security, and other support services to the operating divisions of The Boeing Company. It partners with the operating divisions to provide quality, cost-effective services to meet the company's needs.

The largest portion of ISS support is computing and is managed by the ISS Computing and Network Operations (CNO) organization. This organization performs services for distributed and large-scale computing as well as voice and video support primarily, in the Puget Sound (Washington) area. Its 3,700 Puget Sound employees support over 170,000 distributed computing devices, 60,000 voice mail boxes, and 150,000 phone lines in the Puget Sound area. Other major ISS locations include: Philadelphia, Wichita, and Huntsville.

This case study examines process analysis of Boeing's computing restoration service. The case demonstrates how the Process Analysis Model supported the restoration team through the steps of Identify Component Structure, Establish Measurement Plan, and Trace and Attribute Cross-functional Cost to the Process.

In response to an increasing dependency on its distributed computing services, and rising costs of these services, ISS sought ways to improve its performance using activity-based management.

The current ISS Process Management Initiative for distributed computing services began in 1995. The objective was to develop facts and data to support better decision making within the CNO organization. Specifically, the target of this effort was to guide process improvements to achieve greater total customer satisfaction (quality, cost, delivery, safety, and morale).

First, the set of CNO computing services was defined as: acquisition, computing administration, restoration, relocation, disposition, technical integration and design, large scale (mainframe), voice, and video. With senior management commitment, a dedicated owner was established for each of these services. Additional cross-functional participants were identified to form service analysis teams for each service.

PROCESS ANALYSIS

The Boeing ISS restoration service responds to distributed computing hardware and software problems. The boundaries of this service are presented in Table 12 below. After defining the restoration service's boundaries, the next step was to perform a full process analysis on the service.

Table 12: Process Definitions

- **Process Boundaries**
  - Begins with a request for service (functionality failure)
  - Ends with full functionality of equipment/network
- **Includes**
  - Processes and tools used to provide Restoration Support Services
  - Puget Sound locations, Portland, and Spokane
  - Management of cost, cycle time, defects, and workforce
  - Distributed computing hardware, software, and data communications networks
  - Strategic direction of process teams
- **Excludes**
  - Day-to-day management of any site organization
  - Large Scale Computing
  - Voice & Video

IDENTIFY COMPONENT STRUCTURE

The initial difficulty encountered was coming to an understanding of how the restoration service was to be managed. It became apparent that ISS performed computing restoration in three different components, and the service provided had a different focus among each of these. The components were defined as data network restoration, server system restoration, and work-station restoration. The nature of restoring networks versus servers versus workstations involves separate complexities in managing each of them. The Component structure chart is represented in Figure 10.

Figure 10: Component Structure of Restoration Service

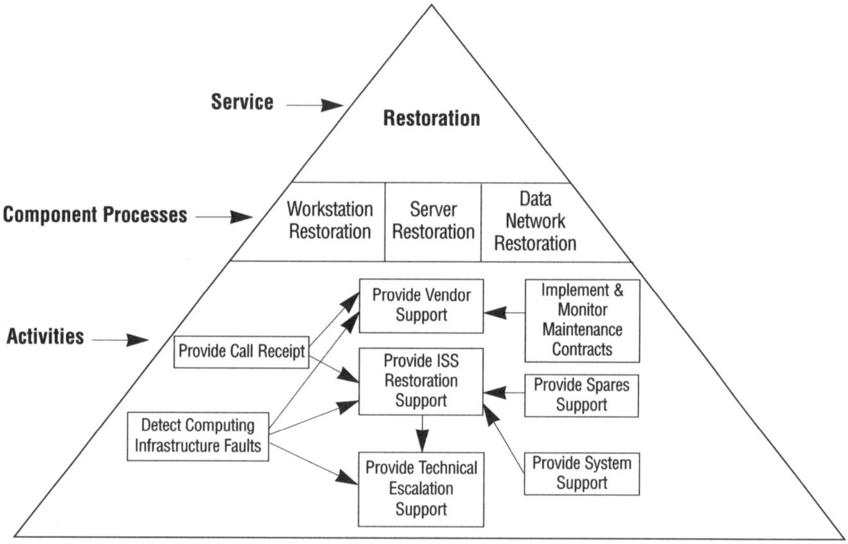

Service
Restoration
Component Processes
Workstation Restoration
Server Restoration
Data Network Restoration
Activities
Provide Call Receipt
Detect Computing Infrastructure Faults
Provide Vendor Support
Provide ISS Restoration Support
Provide Technical Escalation Support
Implement & Monitor Maintenance Contracts
Provide Spares Support
Provide System Support

As noted in Figure 10, the performance of the three component processes is managed by following a set of eight key activities. The first two involve receiving a call for restoration and determining any first level problem resolutions and computing infrastructure faults. The second set of three activities involves assigning a vendor, ISS in-house, or additional technical resources to the problem. The additional technical resources are assigned when the computing problem is overly complex for the vendor and ISS in-house resources to solve. The third set of three activities involves managing the vendor-maintenance contracts, providing spare parts to solve the restoration problem, and managing systems that track and collect restoration service information and assist in restoring the problem.

ESTABLISH MEASUREMENT PLAN

Since the service owner participated on the restoration team, the process step flow was easily verified with the owner. After discovering process information needs, the team shifted their focus to establishing a measurement plan.

The first difficulty in performing this step was that ISS is an internal cost center of The Boeing Company. ISS does not maintain its own revenues and profits as would the Boeing Commercial Airplane Group, for example. This posed a difficulty in identifying financial and non-financial measures that were necessary for managing restoration, because ISS had multiple sets of customers. On one hand, the customers were the ISS management who were responsible for performing computing operations. Other customers were the Boeing divisions to which ISS provided computing services, such as restoration.

In analyzing the service's classification dimensions, restoration is shown to have the characteristics of a service shop. The dimensions are presented below in Table 13.

Table 13: CAM-I Service Classification Grid for Restoration Service

Classification Dimension	Mass Service	Service Shop	Professional Service	Classification Dimension
Equipment focus		•		People focus
Back-office focus		•		Front-office focus
Product focus		•		Process focus
Low level of customization of the service to any one customer			•	High level of customization of the service to any one customer
Minimal discretion available to front office staff			•	Considerable discretion available to front office staff
Minimal contact time available by front office staff		•		Considerable contact time available by front office staff

Once the service was identified as being similar to a service shop, the question, "What measures a successful restoration?" had to be answered. The team determined that five measures were key for managing restoration: defects, cycle time, cost per unit, volume, and efficiency. Defects and cycle time measure the health and speed of providing the restoration service in an attempt at measuring quality. Obviously end users are most concerned with the time it takes for their hardware or software problem to be resolved.

The cost per unit of providing the service is measured to manage the dollar commitment to ISS managers and Boeing divisions. This measure also helps track any productivity gains made through volume and efficiency improvements.

The efficiency measure tracks how many labor hours are needed to perform one restoration. This measure aids in productivity tracking and in forecasting resources when volumes are expected to change. Restoration volumes could change due to new technology introduction, education programs, or service level agreements.

Given the set of measures, how to collect data had to be explored. Non-financial data that were available were a mix of product and process focus. The result was that much of the process data needed to track performance were not readily available. Systems changes had to be made and some manual processes had to be implemented in order to harvest the process data. For example, new processes involving the trouble ticket system had to be developed in order to capture the necessary process data.

One difficulty in establishing sources for the cost data was that the current accounting system did not track costs by service. In other words, few budgets were set up to collect costs for the restoration service. The labor hours needed for the measurements had to be gathered from a quarterly survey of participants in the services. Furthermore, the restoration team found that the measurements had to be reported at the site or unit level rather than at the larger total restoration service level. This was because the work mix at each site was different, as were productivity and resource levels.

The operational definitions of the measures and sources for the measurement data are:

Defects: Lost workstation hours
(impact of computing outages on end users)

Percent of commitments missed
(problems not solved within contracted time)
Source: Trouble/problem ticket system,
equipment management system

Cycle Time: Mean elapsed time to restore problem
Source: Trouble/problem ticket system

Cost Per Unit: Total cross-functional resource costs divided by volume
Source: Accounting system, labor surveys, trouble/problem ticket system

Volume: The number of computing problems, including those resolved by phone (quick tickets) and dispatched problems
Source: Trouble/problem ticket system

Efficiency: Restoration tickets handled per labor hour
Source: Labor surveys, trouble/problem ticket system

TRACE AND ATTRIBUTE CROSS-FUNCTIONAL COST TO THE PROCESS

As mentioned above, a labor survey was implemented to collect labor costs of the participants in the CNO services. The individuals in the ISS organizations that contribute resources to restoration recorded the percent of their time spent on this service. Next, the total hours charged to the accounting system were applied to the survey percentages to estimate hours spent on each service.

The survey helped identify the ISS organizations that contributed resources to restoration, and a process flow audit determined the

Figure 11: Process Model of Restoration Service

Resources

Site Computing Operations
Customer Service Center
Technical Services
Inventory Management
Material Hardware Maintenance
Restoration Computing Systems Management
Supplier Maintenance Performance Management
External Vendor

Activities

Provide Call Receipt & 1st Level Problem Resolution
Detect faults in Distributed Computing Infrastructure
Provide ISS Site Restoration Support
Provide Spares Support
Provide Technical Escalation Support
Implement & Monitor Maintenance
Provide System Support
Provide Vendor Support

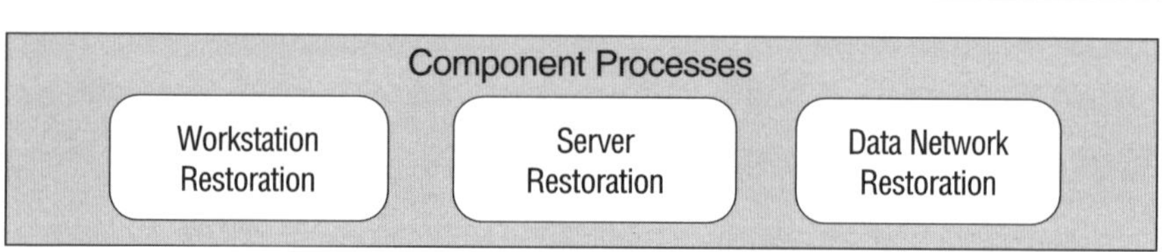

other resources. These other cross-functional resources included external vendor maintenance contracts and inventory management groups. The process model illustrated in Figure 11 reveals all of the resources used in the activities and component processes of the restoration service.

The next step was to trace the cross-functional resource costs to the activities and to the component processes. The labor survey helped accomplish this task, and the volume of restoration problems aided this effort as well. To trace some activity costs to the component processes, the percentage of the total volume that each component incurred was used. For example, in analyzing the provide-technical-escalation-support activity, if server system problems were 10 percent of the total problem volume, then 10 percent of this activity's costs were traced to the server system component process. Other methods involved analyzing accounts payable records to trace resource and activity costs through the process. Examples of tracing resource costs to activities are shown in Figure 12 and 13, and examples of tracing activity cost to component processes are presented in Figure 14 and 15.

Figure 12: Tracing Resource Cost To Activities

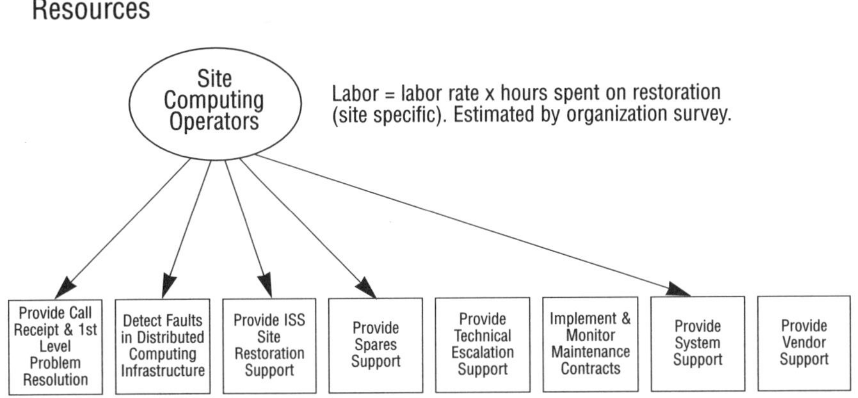

Figure 13: Tracing Resource Cost To Activities

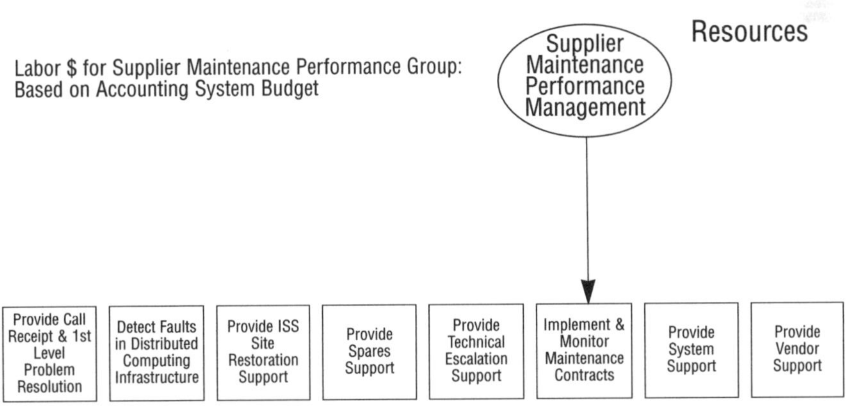

Figure 14: Tracing Resource Cost To Component Processes

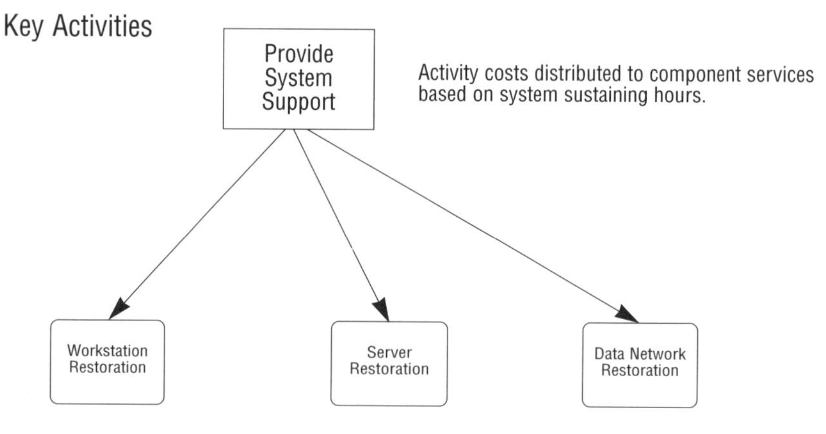

Figure 15: Tracing Resource Cost To Component Processes

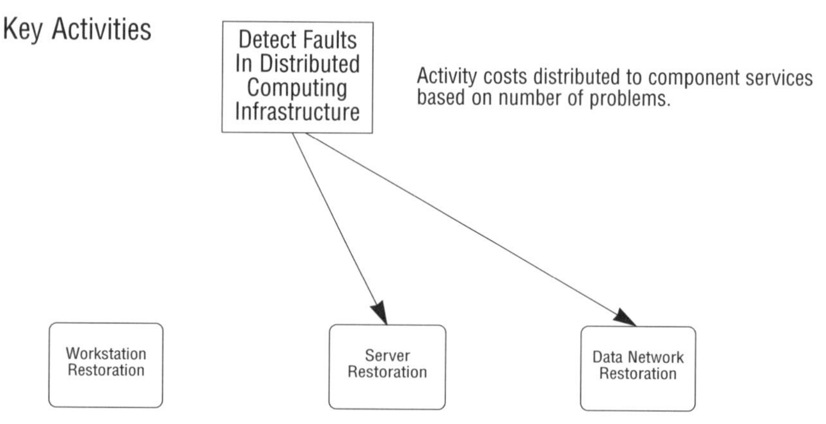

CONCLUSION

The result of the process analysis performed on the ISS restoration service is that process reporting is now available, leading to a basis on which to make better business decisions. The process analysis of restoration gave visibility to improvement activities centered around software maintenance and contract management. By providing cost and non-cost data by site, the process team was able to identify best practices among the sites, as well as to develop improvement plans specific to each site. Useful planning ratios were developed. The transition to an activity-based management approach strengthened line management ownership of site specific data and targets.

The service owner can now monitor service performance, forecast resource levels based on volume fluctuations, and respond to specific customer requests. For example, the customer may be unsatisfied with the current cycle time to solve a restoration problem. ISS can use the process analysis information to determine the amount of resources needed to reduce cycle time, and calculate the expected cost increases or defect fluctuations due to the change. The customer can then decide if the additional cost is affordable in relation to the reduction in cycle time. The Process Analysis Model has prepared the participants to better manage the service.

After tracing and attributing all of the cross-functional costs to the process, the team worked through its data collection method to create credible, actionable information. Cost by resource, cost by activity, and efficiencies were reported monthly for each component process.

Furthermore, the measures established in the measurement plan were reported using a "four-up chart" format as exemplified in Figure 16. This format reports the defect, cycle time, cost, cost per unit, and cycle time measures on the same page. The chart helps the user to more readily see the interaction between the various measures and their impacts on each other. This led to a higher level of process knowledge to allow for process improvement, resource planning and better decision-making for the team.

Figure 16: The Four-Up Chart

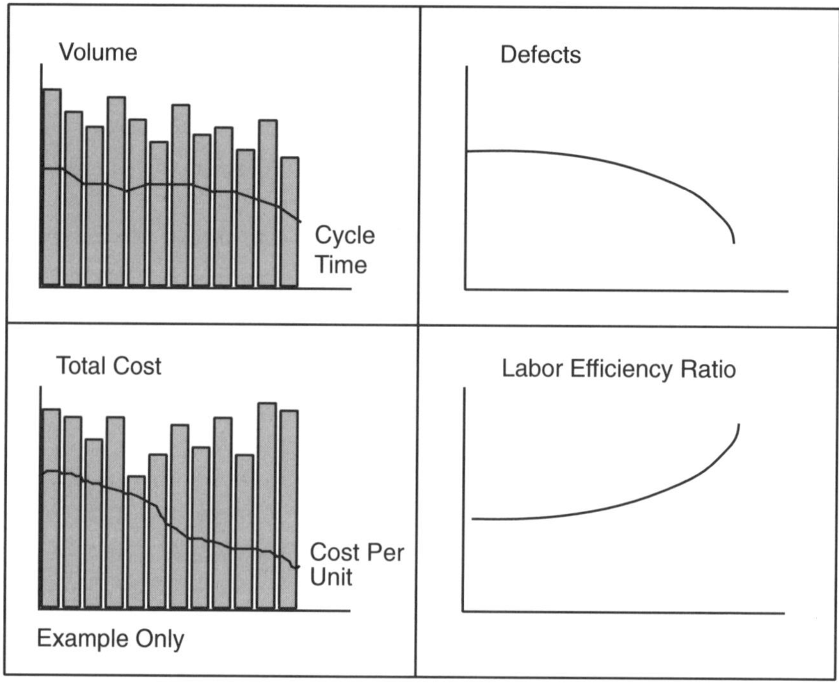

SECTION 5

CAM-I CASE STUDY: GTE Directories Corporation: Measurement Development for Understanding Markets and Customer Requirements

Bruce Rosenstiel
GTE Directories Corporation

BACKGROUND

The GTE Directories case study focuses on the measures established for the Define Customer Needs and Wants sub-process.

GTE Directories is a fully integrated provider of directory advertising, competing in both the hard copy and electronic marketplace. The 61-year-old, billion-dollar-plus operation sells, publishes, prints, and delivers directories in 35 states in the U.S.A. and in several international locations.

The 1984 AT&T break-up, combined with economic downturns and increased competition in important markets, wreaked havoc in what had been an unrelenting growth market. In response to these new pressures, GTE launched a corporate-wide quality initiative in 1986 to focus on quality as the competitive edge. By the late 80s quality was becoming part of the working vocabulary at GTE Directories. In 1991, senior executives, sensing that more was needed, challenged GTE Directories' management to apply for and win the Malcolm Baldrige National Quality Award (MBNQA).

This announcement galvanized the employees to action and helped begin to focus the company on processes rather than on functional cost centers. GTE Directories won the MBNQA for service companies in 1994 on the strength of its customer orientation and quality improvement teams.

During 1995, realizing that the momentum gained during the pursuit of the MBNQA was wearing thin, GTE Directories' new president announced a Best in Class initiative to move the company beyond MBNQA. To meet the new challenge, employees needed to assess their processes, establish appropriate measures, and become more effective process managers.

PROCESS ANALYSIS

In this section, we describe the analytical process used within the "Understand Markets and Customer Requirements" process to develop process measures.

Senior management was committed to managing the organization based on processes. They decided that the 12 generic processes defined in the Arthur Andersen/International Benchmarking Clearinghouse Process Classification Framework adequately represented the processes within GTE Directories. All of the organization's processes were undergoing review to begin the continuous improvement cycle.

As one of the first steps, each of the high-level process teams reviewed the Process Classification Framework (Figure 2) to determine if the sub-processes and activities represented the work performed within each of their areas. For the twelve generic processes to be more clearly understood by employees, the teams mapped their current processes to them. For example, Produce and Deliver encompassed Manage and Produce Ads/Graphics, Manage Listings, Manage Directories, Manage and Produce Pages, and Manage Warehousing and Distribution.

IDENTIFY COMPONENT STRUCTURE

The team (which included customers) discussed and defined the output for the Determine Customer Needs and Wants sub-process in terms that customers understood and used, by answering the following two questions and completing the component structure triangle (Figure 17).

- Who is the customer?

  The process customer is the marketing analyst from sales promotion, product design, or other marketing group who requested that a specific assessment be conducted and will use the information gathered.

- What do they receive?

  The marketing analyst receives detailed and summarized marketing information.

  The output is predictive marketing data.

  The service is customer assessment to predict purchasing behavior.

  The activities that support gathering the raw data are categorized under qualitative and quantitative assessments.

  The activities are: conduct customer interviews, conduct focus groups, develop and implement surveys, and predict purchasing behavior.

Figure 17: Component Structure

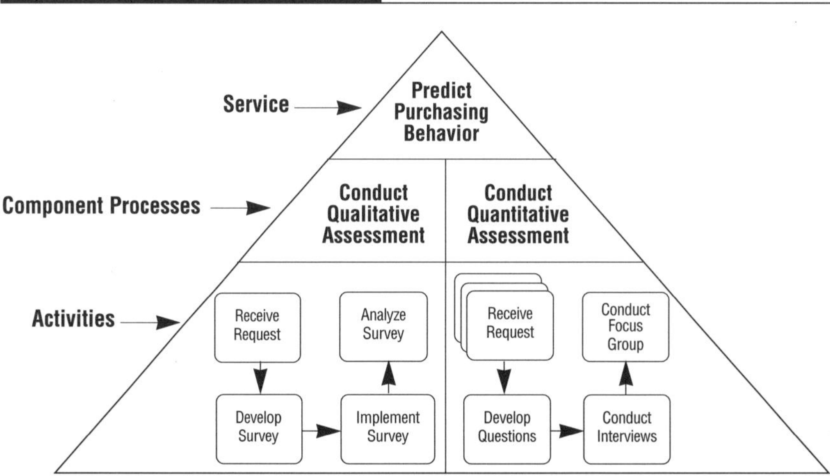

ESTABLISH A MEASUREMENT PLAN

After the service was defined in customer terms and the activities identified and verified, measurements were established.

Service Types and Classification Dimensions

To facilitate establishing measures, the following classification dimension questions were answered.

- Is the process dependent on people or equipment?

  The process is dependent on the interaction of process performers, the market researchers, with the market analyst and the information suppliers (the external customers).

- Is the value to the customer dependent on the interaction with the company's representatives or the company's product?

  Yes, the value the marketing analyst receives is dependent on the delivered internal product of tabulated and raw assessment and predictive information.

- Is the value received from a tangible product or does the customer participate in a service process?

  The value is derived from the quality of the predictive analysis and of the information collected during the assessments. Although the quality attributes may be difficult to measure, the product is tangible.

- Is each iteration, sale, or event unique or customized to the customer?

  The purpose of the assessments and the question content may vary from event to event. However, the customization is normally minimal and within a known range. Depending on the research requested, the market analyst or researcher may choose from a variety of pre-packaged assessments.

- How much time does the interacting personnel have with the customer?

  The market researcher spends a moderate amount of time determining the marketing analyst's requirements to ensure that the interview will meet the objectives.

Restated and summarized, the responses indicate the following:

1. The process is dependent on the interaction of people. The process performer interacts with the customer to determine requirements. The interaction is not dependent on machines or equipment.
2. The process is front-office focused. The customers deal with individuals who add value to and develop the product.
3. The process is product-focused. The objective is producing assessment data and predictive information.
4. The level of customization is moderate. Assessments are often based on already existing question sets, although additional specific questions are also often added. Occasionally, completely new question sets are developed.
5. Discretion and contact time are also rated at a moderate level.

Using this information, we completed Table 14. The information in this grid indicates that the Determine Customer Needs and Wants sub-process is representative of a professional service. It is more highly people-focused than equipment-focused. The level of autonomy is more that of a professional consultant than that of a "clerk." There is latitude for product or service customization. The customer is interested in a product that is the result of personnel interaction. A professional service type indicates that costs can be traced to products or processes if appropriate information is gathered.

Table 14: CAM-I Service Classification Grid for Telecom Enterprises Example

Classification Dimension	Mass Service	Service Shop	Professional Service	Classification Dimension
Equipment focus			•	People focus
Back-office focus			•	Front-office focus
Product focus		•		Process focus
Low level of customization of the service to any one customer		•		High level of customization of the service to any one customer
Minimal discretion available to front office staff			•	Considerable discretion available to front office staff
Minimal contact time available by front office staff			•	Considerable contact time available by front office staff

To identify measures for the "Determine Customer Needs and Wants" sub-process, we first ensured that there were linked measures from the organization to the process and to the sub-process level. To develop measures, we needed to answer the following measurement questions for GTE Directories:

- What is the vision/mission of the organization?

  Growth through 100 percent customer satisfaction

- What is its competitive differentiation?

  The easiest product to use

The answers to the next three questions are presented in Table 15

- What are the organization-level dimensions of performance?
- What are the organization-level measures?
- What are the organization-level performance targets?

PROCESS LEVEL – LINKED TO ORGANIZATION

The answers to the process-level measurement questions linking the sub-process to the organization are:

- How do my processes support/relate to the organization-level dimensions?

  The Understand Markets and Customers process is responsible for determining customer needs and wants, measuring and monitoring consumer and advertiser satisfaction, and for monitoring changes in expectations. GTE Directories has two specific performance dimensions that are dependent on this process: consumer satisfaction and advertiser satisfaction. The process is also linked to the organization-wide cost-effectiveness initiative. All processes must identify failure and implement action plans to eliminate the failure.

- How do my processes support/relate to the organization-level measures?

  The Understand Markets and Customers process will report consumer and advertiser satisfaction measures.

- How can I measure the aspects of my process that relate to the organization-level dimensions of performance and measures?

  The sub-processes and activities within Understand Markets and Customers have the attributes of a professional service. The processes are people-focused with some customization of the survey/research instruments. The actual interaction to gather the information from the supplier is repetitive and usually homogenous to ensure consistency of results. The process outputs of survey results and satisfaction levels may vary in size and scope, but they are tangible.

Table 15: Dimensions of Performance, Measures, and Performance Targets

Dimensions	Measures	Performance Targets
Revenue Growth	(Current year revenue - prior year revenue) / prior year revenue	6.5 %
Cost Effectiveness	(Total Cost - Cost of Failure) / Total Cost	75%
Financial Performance	Net Income	$ 145 M
Consumer Satisfaction	Percent of consumers answering excellent or good on satisfaction survey	95%
Advertiser Satisfaction	Percent of advertisers answering excellent and good on satisfaction survey	88%
Advertiser Growth	(Number of current year advertisers – number of prior year advertisers) / divided by prior year advertisers	10%
Employee Turnover	Number of employees leaving the company / [(number of employees at the beginning of the year + the number of employees at the end of the year)/2]	22 %
Customer Complaints	Number of complaints/ Number of customers	2%
Shareholder Value	Dividends received + stock appreciation	10%

NOTE: Numbers are for example only, and do not represent actual performance targets.

The customer-focused, process-level measurement questions are:

- What do my customers value?

  The market analysts value accuracy, reliability, and timeliness of the information provided from the three sub-processes: Determine Customer Needs and Wants, Measure Customer Satisfaction, and Monitor Changes in Market or Customer Expectations. The organization values the efficiency of the sub-processes and cost effectiveness of external suppliers.

- How can I measure what my customers value?

  The service quality characteristics that the market analyst stated they value are: accuracy, reliability, and timeliness (which can be viewed as product reliability), process responsiveness, and process delivery speed. Market analysts are concerned with the reliability of the information collected (the product of the process). Was the sample statistically valid? Was the research conducted in a manner consistent with previous samples? Were the research instruments validated? Each of these components can be measured.

Market analysts are also concerned with how quickly the information is gathered after our competitors' product launch and how soon the information is available for the semi-annual satisfaction sampling. An objective can be established for "statistically valid research to be conducted within XX days of launch with information to be available within YY days." This objective provides both process responsiveness and delivery speed.

An objective was also established to "conduct statistically valid research for all products on a semi-annual basis during June and December of each year. The information will be available for the market analyst within 15 days of research completion."

Cost effectiveness can be measured by analyzing value-added and non-value-added activities within the process and applying time and cost measures to them. Time data will be collected monthly through project time reporting. Each research event will be treated as a separate project and participants will track their time in half-hour increments. Costs will be applied based on percent of time. Non-value-added activities include all re-work and invalidated samples. Cost effectiveness for each supplier will be measured by tracking supplier cost for the various types of research and for each project.

The answers to the measurement questions addressing balance at the process level are:

- Do these measures provide for a balanced view of my processes?

  Yes. The quality measures balance speed of delivery with statistical reliability. The cost-effectiveness measures focus on doing the process right the first time and on evaluating each supplier based on the value received from each.

- What additional measures would provide a more balanced view?

  Employee satisfaction is measured at an organization level. If the responses are below normal for specific processes, employee satisfaction will be adopted as a process measurement.

- What additional information do I need to manage the organization/process?

  The relationship of successful new product offerings with the sub-process may identify innovations that meet customer needs and provide an indication of process effectiveness. The measures to capture are: number of new innovations identified and submitted to design products and services, and number of new well- received products and services.

- Do I need to be able to support other initiatives (e.g., CPI, TQM, ABC/M, pricing strategies, supply chain management)?

  No. The organization is currently focusing on continuous process improvement and Best in Class initiatives in customer satisfaction, employee satisfaction, and cost effectiveness. The cost-effectiveness measurement has already been identified. The "Understand Markets and Customers" process does not directly affect the current customer satisfaction measure.

The answers to the measurement questions addressing practicality at the process level are:

- Do I have tracking systems in place?

  Yes and no. We currently track the number of surveys implemented and the number of interviews and focus groups conducted. The survey and interview questions are validated through the American Society for Quality (ASQ). Five years of survey objectives, questions, and results are kept to ensure comparability of results. We are not currently tracking time and resources associated with each project. We do not track output and supplier costs that allow ready correlation and value determination.

- Is it cost effective to develop the tracking system(s)?

  Yes. It would be simple to require the employees involved in research activities to manually track their time by project and to provide that information on a monthly basis. A template could be developed on an electronic spreadsheet and distributed to ensure consistent reporting. Supplier invoices can be coded to each project and costs-per-project-per-supplier reported from accounts payable. The value received would be determined by comparing the number of surveys/focus groups/interviews conducted versus cost.

- Which measures that I am already tracking meet the new requirements?

  The process and product quality measures are in place.

- Which measures will I retire with the implementation of the new measures?

  None. The measures used for this process are all necessary.

TRACE AND ATTRIBUTE CROSS-FUNCTIONAL COST TO THE PROCESS

Since cost information will be collected for each research project, costs can be traced to the product when the research is specific to that product. When the research is broader in scope — for example, encompassing product families, product packaging, interaction with sales representatives, brand recognition — costs should be assigned to the appropriate hierarchical level such as market, customer, channel, or organization.

RESULTS

Based on the above analysis, new measures were established to ensure that the process was cost effective and met the market analysts' requirements. Table 16 indicates where the measures will occur and for which performance dimensions.

CONCLUSION

The use of the Business Process Relationship Map to frame and identify the processes/activities will make future external benchmarking easier. The component structure helped the team focus on the appropriate level of detail. The results of the service process classification grid confirmed the professional service orientation of the process, which enabled appropriate selection of measures, while responding to the performance measures questions. Information is still being gathered and analyzed. Changes have not yet been made to the process based on the information reported.

Table 16: CAM-I Process Measurement Matrix

CAM-I Process Framework Measurement Matrix	Service Type				Dimension of Performance		
Process, Sub-process, Activity from the IBC Process Classification	**Mass Services**	**Service Shop**	**Profes-sional Services**	**Financial Perform-ance**	**Quality**	**Flexibility**	**Resource Utilization**
Understand Markets and Customers			•	X	X	X	X
Determine customer needs and wants			•				
Conduct qualitative assessments			•				
Conduct customer interviews			•	X	X	X	X
Conduct focus groups			•	X	X	X	X
Conduct quantitative assessments			•				
Develop and implement surveys		•		X	X	X	X
Predict customer purchasing behavior			•		X	X	X

KEY: • Service Type
X Performance Dimension

SECTION 6

CAM-I CASE STUDY: The United States Marine Corps: Re-Engineering the Resource Allocation Process

Captain Thomas Peck
USMC

> "End state is a re-engineered process focused on securing adequate resources needed to sustain Marine Corps warfighting capability."
>
> General C. C. Krulak
> Commandant, U.S. Marine Corps

OVERVIEW

The Marine Corps case study takes a look at how a government agency used the service process methodology. The Marine Corps is required to respond to resource and policy-related inquires from other military services and external agencies such as Congress and the Office of the Secretary of Defense. Re-engineering this process to obtain the "best, most timely" answer to these requests became one of the Corps' highest priorities. The case study examines how to use both the business process relationship map and the component services structure triangle to help identify the key activities within the process. Since the Marine Corps is not a for-profit organization, establishing a measurement plan was more difficult. This case study focuses on measuring non-financial performance such as reduced cycle time and improved quality. The implications of process change and the end result of the process review are also discussed.

BACKGROUND

The Marine Corps Continuous Process Improvement Program (MCCPIP) began in May 1995 as an outgrowth from the combat development process (CDP) functional process improvement initiative. The MCCPIP encompasses a comprehensive evaluation of critical processes within the Corps, with primary emphasis on core business processes at the headquarters level. The MCCPIP objectives are directed at improving the effectiveness and efficiency of these processes with the ultimate goal of significant improvements in productivity, reduced cycle time, and cost reductions. Given the Commandant's guidance that "resourcing the Corps" was a top priority, the resource allocation process became the first of eight core business processes to be targeted for process improvement.

With senior management already committed to process improvement, the next step involved identifying process owners. Effective in November 1995, the Deputy Chief of Staff for Programs and Resources (DC/S P&R) was given total responsibility for all Marine Corps planning, programming, and budgeting matters. This decision by General Krulak ensured: 1) comprehensive and consistent resource priorities across all phases of the planning, programming, and budgeting processes, 2) focused and efficient efforts toward Corps resource allocation, and 3) a clear, consistent message to all external resource interfaces (Congress, the Department of Defense, and the Department of the Navy).

Re-engineering the resource allocation process identified three key performance objectives:

- Develop and maintain the organizational adaptability required to minimize response time and provide the best answer to external initiatives.
- Exceed the information management and analytical capabilities of the competition.

- Ensure a resource strategy that maintains or increases the Corps' total share of the defense budget while maintaining its emphasis on combat development.

In scheduling these objectives, many different sub-process improvements were enacted — all designed to streamline and to provide greater visibility, accountability, and finally greater discipline to the resource allocation process. It is the effort to achieve the first objective of the "best, most timely" answer that this case study will examine.

THE INQUIRY RESPONSE PROCESS: AN "AS-IS" VIEW

The Marine Corps is required to respond to resource and policy-related inquiries from its customers — other services and external agencies, (e.g., Congress, Office of the Secretary of Defense). Many of these inquiries are time-sensitive in nature and require the active participation of headquarters staff organizations. This headquarters organization involves several layers of sponsors and organizations that are responsible for various portions of the inquiry. Many of these are not physically located in the immediate vicinity.

Given the level of effort spent responding to these inquiries and their high visibility/importance, improving the inquiry response process became a high priority target. While the current process was not "broken," there were definitely process improvement opportunities. With senior management committed to this effort, a process improvement team was formed with the charter to re-engineer the inquiry response process.

PROCESS ANALYSIS METHOD

Identifying the Component Structure

After reviewing their roles and responsibilities and developing a plan, the working group's first major milestone was identifying the component structure. The difficulty with this activity is in defining the service output in terms of the customers and balancing that perspective with how it will be managed within the enterprise. Additionally, as pointed out in this manual, linking the operational processes and the management and support processes was quite a challenge. As the Process Relationship Map indicates in Figure 5 (page 7), there are some activities that can be traced to operational processes and others that cannot. Attempts to develop these linkages

Figure 18: The U.S. Marine Corps Process Relationship Map

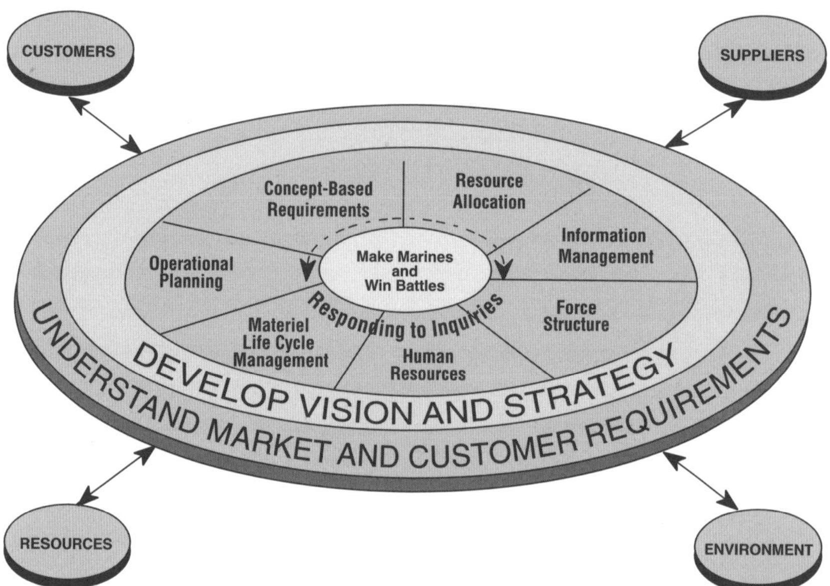

can be shown using both the Process Relationship Map (Figure 5, page 7) and the Component Structure Triangle (Figure 7, page 13).

As Figure 18, indicates, the center of the Corps' process relationship map is the key operational process, or output, of making Marines and winning battles. This is what the Corps' primary customer, the American public, expects of them. Key process improvement opportunities lie in the eight core processes (or support processes), such as the resource allocation process, that surround the center circle and support the Marine Corps' mission of making Marines and winning battles. One of the many sub-processes that provide a common thread throughout all of these processes is the inquiry response process. While directly linked to the resource allocation process because quicker, better responses will likely result in proper funding, this sub-process also impacts all of the core processes and ultimately impacts the ability to make Marines and win battles. It is

Figure 19: Component Service Structure – The Marine Corps Inquiry Response Process

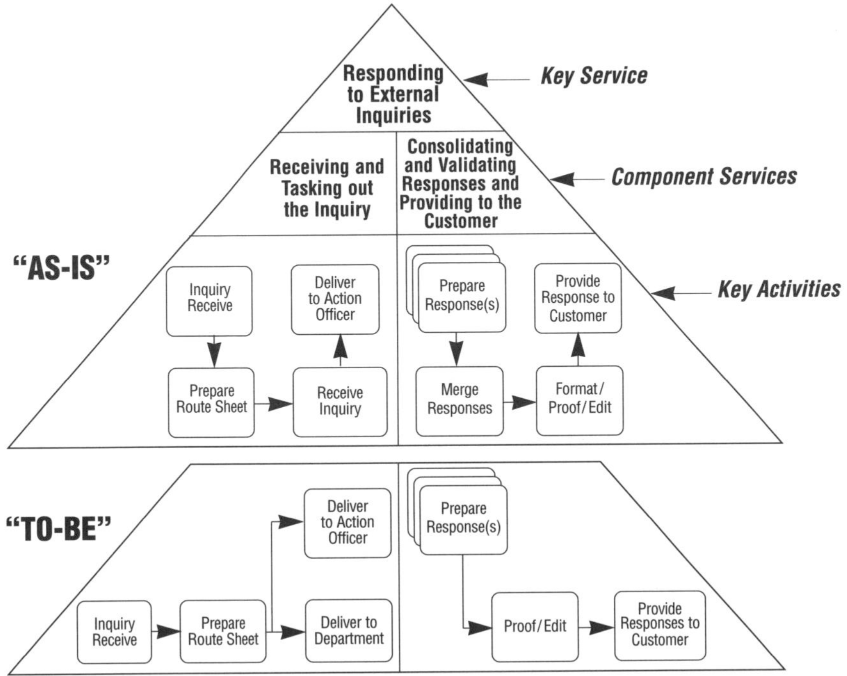

this linkage between the Corps' mission and the support processes and sub-processes that has been missing from previous re-engineering models. The difficulty in this analysis lies in the fact that, although the customer is clearly defined, prior to now, the process itself was not clearly defined and boundaries were ill-defined at best.

Switching to the Component Services Structure Triangle shown in Figure 19, at the top of the triangle is "responding to external inquiries" – a key service from the customer's perspective. The re-engineering team will focus on the bottom two levels of the triangle, all of the components and activities necessary to deliver this service to the customer. Responding to external inquiries can be broken into two key components: receiving and routing the inquiries (i.e., taskers) and consolidating and validating responses to those taskers. It is the activities within these components that provided the process analysis challenge.

The "old" or "As-Is" inquiry response process involved receiving a hardcopy list of questions/issues. Many times these had to be picked up at the Pentagon, which is a half mile from Marine headquarters. These questions were then tasked out using a hand-typed route sheet and passed to the appropriate department for action. Using the top-down mentality, it was often several hours before the department head had sub-tasked the questions through the chain of command and eventually to the action officer.

Geography added additional stress to the process, as many questions needed to be routed to Quantico, Virginia, thirty miles to the south. Additionally, it was often unclear who was responsible for which taskers, as roles and responsibilities often overlapped and were not well understood. Perhaps most important, however, was the effort required to ensure the Marine Corps was speaking with one constant voice. Action officers were not sure if this was always happening. This combination of immediate taskers, geographic restrictions, and lack of clarity often resulted in action officers being cheated out of several hours and possibly a day or two of preparing their response. This clearly inhibited the goal of a "best, most timely answer."

Consolidating and validating responses presented its own problems. Responses to taskers were often delayed because of the same geographic separation. They often came back in no specific order, and different formats and instructions are used by each customer. Programs and Resources Department or the Office of Legislative Affairs personnel were then charged with merging and collating them, ensuring the responses were in the correct format, and proofreading and editing them prior to releasing the responses back to the customer. Responses were also validated to ensure they were consistent with the President's budget and previous responses. The challenges were clear. The team now needed to focus on measuring the activities in this process.

ESTABLISH A MEASUREMENT PLAN

After verifying the process steps and auditing the process flow, the next major activity was to establish a measurement plan. Given that the very nature of a service process creates difficulties in defining data, it was a major challenge to identify financial and non-financial measures for the inquiry response process. For example, what are the measures for a promptly and properly completed inquiry response? An obvious answer is respect, credibility, and a properly funded Marine Corps. But how do you measure the service of routing and consolidating inquiry responses? Performance targets and other measurements needed to be identified and developed to help ensure that both efficiency and customer satisfaction targets were met.

To facilitate establishing these measures, the process needed to be differentiated in terms of the classification dimensions in Table 17, which assisted in tracing activity costs. Classifying the service type allowed the Marine Corps to recognize a commonality of issues, problems, and processes, which enabled similar measures to be used and external benchmarking to occur. Applying the questions in Table 4, we find that the Marine Corps' inquiry response process combines the features of mass service, a service shop, and professional services. While the process focuses on the external, tangible product (the response), it is the process of routing and responding to that inquiry and the human interaction of those involved that offered improvement opportunities.

Table 17: CAM-I Service Classification Grid for USMC Example

Classification Dimension	Mass Service	Service Shop	Professional Service	Classification Dimension
Equipment focused			•	People focus
Back-office focus			•	Front-office focus
Product focus		•		Process focus
Low level of customization of the service to any one customer			•	High level of customization of the service to any one customer
Minimal discretion available to front office staff	•			Considerable discretion available to front office staff
Minimal contact time available by front office staff		•		Considerable contact time available by front office staff

Since the Marine Corps is not a for-profit organization, establishing a measurement plan was more difficult. The measures for achieving our goal of the "best" answer were: 1) determining the increased respect or credibility generated towards the Marine Corps on Capitol Hill, and 2) measuring the degree to which the Marine Corps is properly funded. Both of these measures are somewhat subjective in nature. The "most timely" portion of our goal was measured by: 1) the percentage of responses completed on-time, 2) reduced delivery time, 3) reduced cycle time, and 4) reduced level of effort. Through process automation, our goal was to reduce cycle time, or the beginning-to-end effort, per inquiry and response. A lower level of total effort should reduce costs and/or allow employees to do other things, thus resulting in greater overall efficiency.

TRACE AND ATTRIBUTE CROSS-FUNCTIONAL COST TO THE PROCESS

With the key activities identified and the measurement plan established, the third major activity in the process analysis methodology is to trace and attribute cross-functional costs to the process. Since the inquiry response process is people-based, tracing costs is much easier to accomplish. While there is no formal time-reporting system established for measuring effort level in this area, traceability was enhanced through activity-based management. What was found is that Marine headquarters is involved in external interfaces for resourcing purposes and that this level of effort amounts to roughly 10 percent of the entire Marine Corps effort. More specifically, the Corps spends over 2 percent of its total effort participating in the budget review process, of which responding to inquiries is a major activity. This 2 percent effort level involves approximately 130 full-time workers at an annual estimated cost of $8.3 million. Another cost of the "As-Is" process was lost work hours due to slow delivery of the inquiries. Since the inquiry had to be answered by the assigned due date, many civilian employees often had to work over-time, which increased labor costs.

THE END RESULT: THE "TO-BE" PROCESS

After carefully analyzing the process and collecting data and performance measures, the working group came up with several ideas to improve the process. The new and improved key activities are shown in the "To-Be" portion of Figure 8. The end result was the "Inquiry Response System" (IRS). IRS is an electronic routing and responding system for inquires. A Lotus Notes database, IRS electronically routes inquires simultaneously to both the lowest-level action officer and the entire chain of command. This routing is done via electronic mail with a document link to the inquiry. Concurrent routing ensures that everyone is informed; electronic delivery provides quicker delivery and removes the geographic boundaries found in the "old" process.

IRS is based on the concept of a topical index. When the inquiry is loaded into the system, the type of inquiry determines the path it follows while the topic assigned to that inquiry determines the individuals inside that path. For example, an inquiry on "jet aircraft"from the House Appropriations Committee would be routed automatically to a different path and set of users than a question on "family programs" from the Senate Armed Services Committee. Response preparation and response approvals/disapprovals are also done inside the system and a complete work history is maintained.

IRS also features preloaded response templates, which standardize fonts, formats, and margins. Since each customer requires different products, this feature enables users to focus on the content and not administrative details. With a complete archive of past responses and a link to other databases and reference material, IRS also enables the Marine Corps to speak with one voice. It is "one-stop-shopping" for information.

IRS rolled out in February 1997 with over 300 initial users throughout the Washington, D.C. area. Version 2.0 and 2.1 have also subsequently been implemented. The number of users now exceeds 750, and use has expanded throughout northern Virginia. The results have been outstanding. There is upwards of a fourfold reduction in delivery time, which gives action officers more time to respond to inquiries. Faster delivery time combined with the other automated features of the new process has also resulted in over 50 percent of the users stating that their workload has been reduced by 25 percent or more. The quality of the product is up and that has in turn helped our credibility with the customer. But most importantly, our goals of "best, most timely" answer have been met.

OVERCOMING THE BARRIERS TO CHANGE

Implementing a new automated system and changing the mindset of people did not come without its challenges. Managing change is an important part of any process improvement. The project team anticipated problems associated with a steep learning curve, upgrading hardware and software of all users in a timely fashion, and general resistance to a change that would require monitoring a computer system rather than an inbox full of paper. The most important part of implementation was getting senior leadership behind the effort. Early briefs and demonstrations were used to highlight the benefits of the new system and process. Second, a working group representing all users took an active role in re-engineering the process. This "buy-in" or sense of process ownership was critical in passing positive feedback to the actual users of the system. These users were provided hands-on training, a user guide, and quick reference handouts. The key to effectively implementing this system was ensuring that the user was properly trained and provided timely technical support when needed. Common characteristics of those users who did not rate the system as at least a "good" tool were lack of training, no user guide, lack of a pentium processor, lack of computer skills, and non-daily users of the system who never received enough real live hands-on. As new users continue to be added, overcoming these barriers will continue to be our challenge.

CONCLUSION

Government in general, and the Department of Defense in particular, is caught up in a phenomenon of the new information age. The sheer speed with which transactions are now conducted is dramatically affecting how organizations operate and demands a level of adaptability and responsiveness never required in the past. Using this new technology, however, facilitates a more consistent and credible underpinning to all Marine Corps resource initiatives and significantly strengthens Marine Corps competitiveness during a period of increasingly constrained fiscal resources. As these benefits begin to accrue, the Corps will become progressively more prepared for the increasing demands related to declining resources and intensified customer demands.

REFERENCES

Arthur Anderson & Co. and the International Benchmarking Clearinghouse, *Process Classification Framework*, 1993.

The American Productivity and Quality Center and CAM-I, *Activity-Based Management: A Survey of Best Practices.* Houston: American Productivity and Quality Center, 1995.

CAM-I Process Management Interest Group, *CAM-I Process Management Guide.* Bedford: CAM-I, 1996.

Chang, Richard and Paul De Young, *Measuring Organizational Improvement Impact.* Irvine: Richard Chang Associates, Inc, 1995.

Fitzgerald, Lin., Interview. September 15, 1997.

Fitzgerald, Lin, Robert Johnson, Stan Brignall, Rhian Silvestro, and Christopher Voss, *Performance Measurement in Service Businesses.* London: CIMA. 1991.

Heskett, James L., W. Earl Sasser, and Leonard A. Schlesinger. *The Service Profit Chain: How Leading Companies Link Profit and Growth to Loyalty, Satisfaction, and Value.* New York: Free Press, 1997.

Hronec, Steven M., V*ital Signs: Using Quality, Time, and Cost Performance Measurements to Chart Your Company's Future.* Chicago: Arthur Andersen & Co. 1993.

Kaplan, Robert. and David T. Norton., "Using the Balanced Score Card as a Strategic Management System," *Harvard Business Review,* January - February, 1996.

SERVICE PROCESS REVIEW CHECKLIST

SERVICE PROCESS REVIEW CHECKLIST

Project/Process to be reviewed	
Project Leader	

Step 1. Identify Level of Support

	Name	Supportive of Effort?		
Service Owner		Y	N	N/A
Senior Manager		Y	N	N/A

Step 2. For Process Analysis Team

A. Team Members (Should Represent all functional organizations within the service Boundaries)

Functional Organization	Team Member

B. Charter/Goals: ______________________________

C. Action Plan/Milestone: ______________________

Step 3. Identify Component Structure

A. Services
B. Components
C. Activities

Step 4. Identify Process Information Needs

Step 5. Establish Measurement Plan

A. Complete Service Classification Grid
B. Identify Measures

Step 6. Conduct Labor Activity Analysis

Step 7. Trace & Attribute Cross Functional Cost to the Process

Is the service cost material? If no, stop. If yes, continue to Step 8.

Step 8. Provide Feedback that Captures Process Changes

The Boeing Four-Up Chart in an excellent example.

Step 9. Implement Service Management Reporting

COPIES OF SELECTED FIGURES AND TABLES

Figure 2: Process Classification Framework

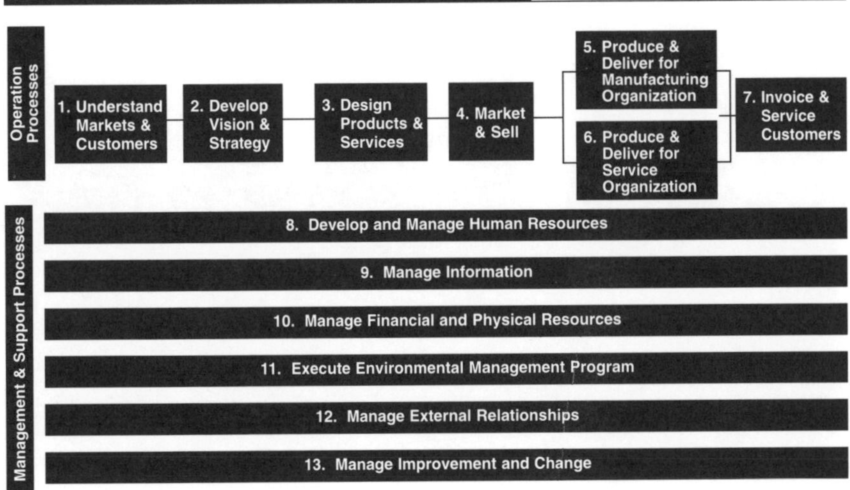

Source: Arthur Andersen, 1993

Figure 5: Process Relationship Map

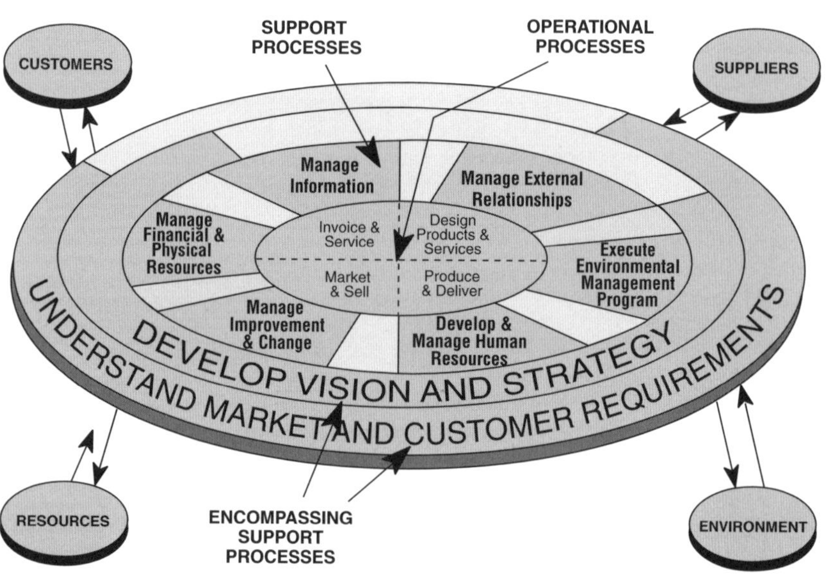

Dark Area = Traceable Costs to Operational Processes
Light Area = Non-Traceable Costs to Operational Processes

Table 1: Service Structure Questions

QUESTION	Answers For A Service Process	Answers For A Manufacturing Process
1. Is the process defined sufficiently to communicate boundaries, inputs, outputs, customers, and suppliers?	Since services may be taken for granted or not be readily apparent, they have not been defined. Significant attention to defining services may not have been a priority. Definitions may need to be created.	Analyses of manufacturing processes have called for definitions to be created so that responsibilities are known.
2. How will process information support your ability to make effective decisions in managing your process?	The different ways that the services are performed may not be known. The provider may not understand how they want to manage the process. What seems to be a single service may require multiple processes. A restaurant may have different processes for washing pots and pans versus dishes. A mover may use different processes for moving and re-connecting computers versus desks.	Different methods of producing the output are known. Management already knows how decisions affect resource allocations.
3. Do you understand the Process?	The activities have not been identified because the service has not been defined as stated above.	The activities are identified and documented.

Figure 6: Service Process Interest Group Analysis Model

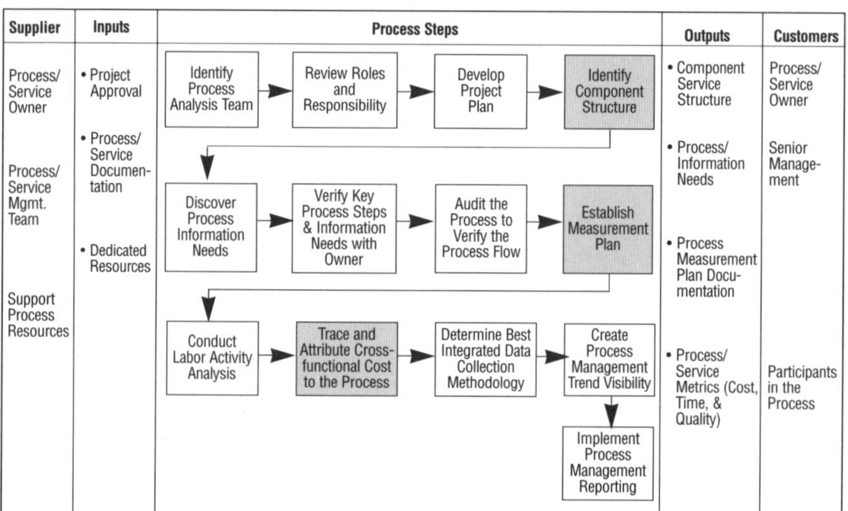

Figure 7: Component Structure Triangle

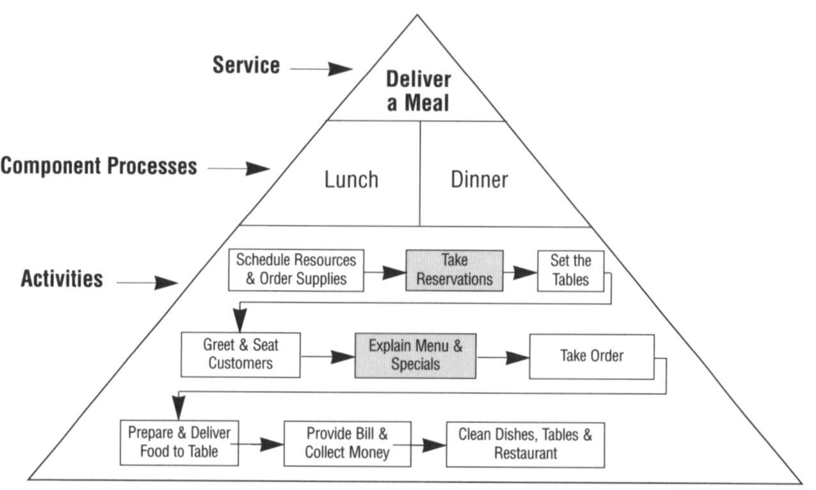

{ Shaded activities are part of the dinner process and not the lunch process }

Table 3: CAM-I Service Classification Grid

Classification Dimension	Mass Service	Service Shop	Professional Service	Classification Dimension
Equipment focus				People focus
Back-office focus				Front-office focus
Product focus				Process focus
Low level of customization of the service to any one customer				High level of customization of the service to any one customer
Minimal discretion available to front office staff				Considerable discretion available to front office staff
Minimal contact time available by front office staff				Considerable contact time available by front office staff

Table 6: Dimensions of Performance and Types of Measures

	DIMENSIONS OF PERFORMANCE	TYPES OF MEASURES
RESULTS	Competitiveness	Relative market share and position Sales growth Measure of the customer base
	Financial performance	Profitability Liquidity Capital Structure Market Ratios
DETERMINANTS	Quality of service	Reliability Responsiveness Aesthetics/appearance Cleanliness/tidiness Comfort Friendliness Communication Courtesy Competence Access Availability Security
	Flexibility	Volume flexibility Delivery speed flexibility Specification flexibility
	Resource utilization	Productivity Efficiency
	Innovation	Performance of the innovation process Performance of individual innovations

Source: Fitzgerald et al., 1991, p. 8

Table 7: CAM-I Process Measurement Matrix (PMM)

	Service Type			Dimension of Performance			
Process, Sub-process, Activity from the IBC Process Classification Framework	Mass Services	Service Shop	Professional Services	Financial Performance	Quality	Flexibility	Resource Utilization
PRODUCE AND DELIVER MEALS							
Plan for and acquire necessary resources or inputs							
Acquire capital goods (restaurant, stoves, computer)							
Hire employees							
Obtain materials and supplies (cooking, cleaning)							
Obtain appropriate technology							
Convert resources or inputs into products							
Develop and adjust production process							
Schedule production (breads, soups, food prep)							
Move materials and resources							
Make product (meals)							
Package and store the product (if appropriate)							
Stage the product for delivery (move to counter)							
Make delivery							
Arrange product shipment (delivery)							
Deliver products to customers (table service)							
Install (if specified)							
Manage produce and deliver process							
Document and monitor order status							
Manage inventories (frozen, pre-packaged, daily)							
Assure quality Schedule and perform maintenance (cleaning)							
Monitor environmental constraints (EPA, FDA)							

Table 8: Performance Measurement Questions

Organization Level - data to gather rather than questions to answer

- What is the vision / mission of the organization?
- What is the organization's unique competency?
- What are the organization-level dimensions of performance?
- What are the organization-level measures?
- What are the organization-level performance targets?

Process Level

Linked to Organization (Not all are necessarily linked/related to your processes)

- How do my processes support/relate to the organization-level dimensions of performance?
- How do my processes support/relate to the organization-level measures?
- How can I measure the aspects of my process that relate to the organization-level dimensions of performance and measures? (The answer is partially dependent on the service-type and segregation qualities.)

Customer Focused

- What do my customers value?
- How can I measure what my customers' value? (The answer is partially dependent on the service-type and segregation qualities.)

Balancing

- Do these measures provide for a balanced view of my processes?
- What additional measures would provide a balanced view?
- What additional information do I need to manage the organization/process?
- Do I need to be able to support other initiatives (CPI, TQM, ABC/M, Pricing strategies, Supply Chain Management, etc.)?

Practicality

- Do I have tracking systems in place?
- Is it cost effective to develop the tracking system(s)?
- Which measures that I am already tracking meet the new requirements?
- Which measures will I retire with the implementation of the new measures?

Table 9: Restaurant Dimensions of Performance, Measures and Performance Targets at the Organizational Level

Dimension of Performance	Types of Measures	Key Measures	Performance Targets
Financial Performance	*Revenue Growth*	(Current year revenue - prior year revenue) / prior year revenue	6.5 %
Financial Performance	*Cost effectiveness*	Spoiled ingredients / Gross ingredients	5 %
Financial Performance	*Net Income*	Revenue – Expenses	$145,000
Quality of Service	*Customer* Satisfaction	Percent of repeat credit card users to total credit card users	75 %
Competitiveness	*Customer Growth*	(Number of current year customers – number of prior year customers) / prior year customers	15%
Resource Utilization	*Employee Satisfaction*	Percent of employees who respond excellent or good on the employee opinion survey	80%
Resource Utilization	*Employee Turnover*	Number of employees leaving the company / [(number of employees at the beginning of the year + the number of employees at the end of the year)/2]	25 %
Quality of Service	*Customer Complaints*	Number of complaints / number of customers	2 %

Table 11: Cost Tracing Preconditions and Concerns

Service Type	Resource	Data Source	Data Source/Method
Mass	Equipment	Equipment/maintenance General ledger labor costs	Off-the-books equipment, records or estimation
	Labor	General ledger labor costs traced to the service by survey/estimation	Service/scheduling systems data used to trace labor hours to the service
	Other non-labor	General ledger non-labor costs	Off-the-books records or estimation
Service shop	Labor	Combination of on and off-the-books- labor collection systems	Survey for estimated times
	Non-labor	Combination of General Ledger non-labor costs and off-the-book estimation	
Professional Service	Labor	General Ledger labor costs timesheets	Operational labor collection records
	Non-labor	General ledger non-labor	Operational non-labor collection records

Figure 8: Process Model

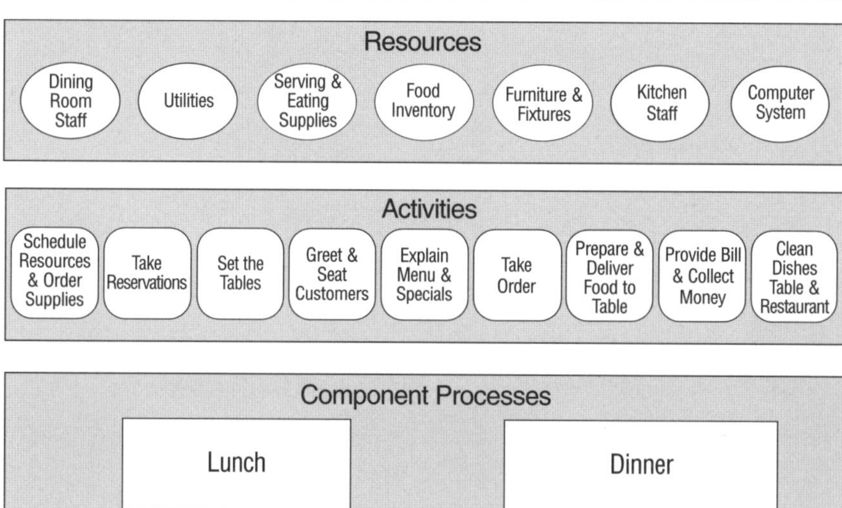

Figure 9: Elements of the Service Process Analysis

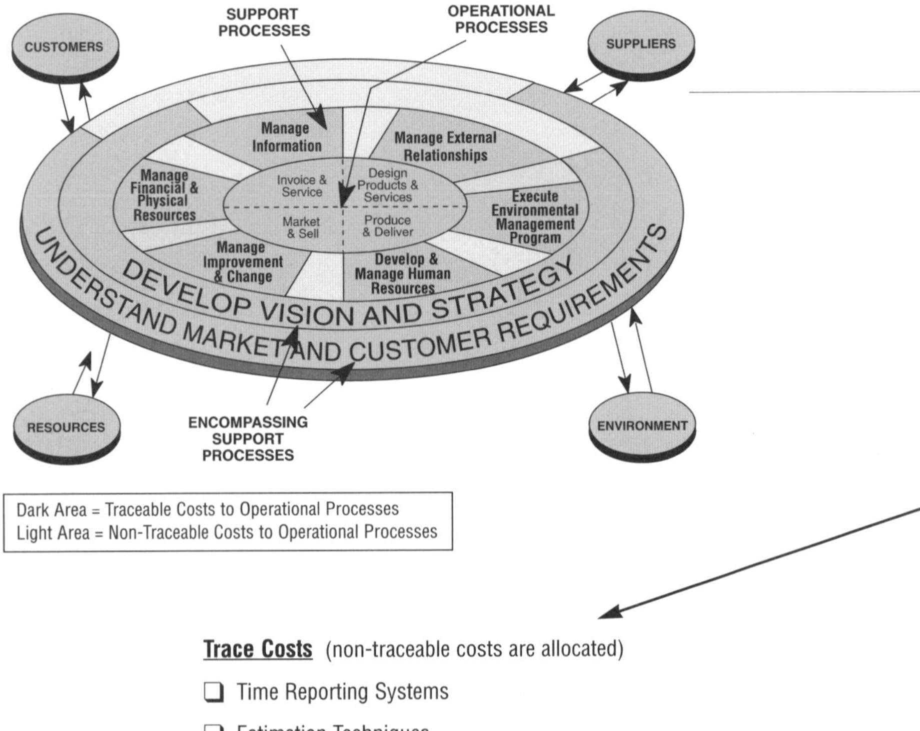

Dark Area = Traceable Costs to Operational Processes
Light Area = Non-Traceable Costs to Operational Processes

Trace Costs (non-traceable costs are allocated)

- ❑ Time Reporting Systems
- ❑ Estimation Techniques
- ❑ Financial Systems
- ❑ ABC
- ❑ Other

Classification Dimension	Mass Service	Service Shop	Professional Service	Classification Dimension
Equipment focus				People focus
Back-office focus				Front-office focus
Product focus				Process focus
Low level of customization of the service to any one customer				High level of customization of the service to any one customer
Minimal discretion available to front office staff				Considerable discretion available to front office staff
Minimal contact time available by front office staff				Considerable contact time available by front office staff

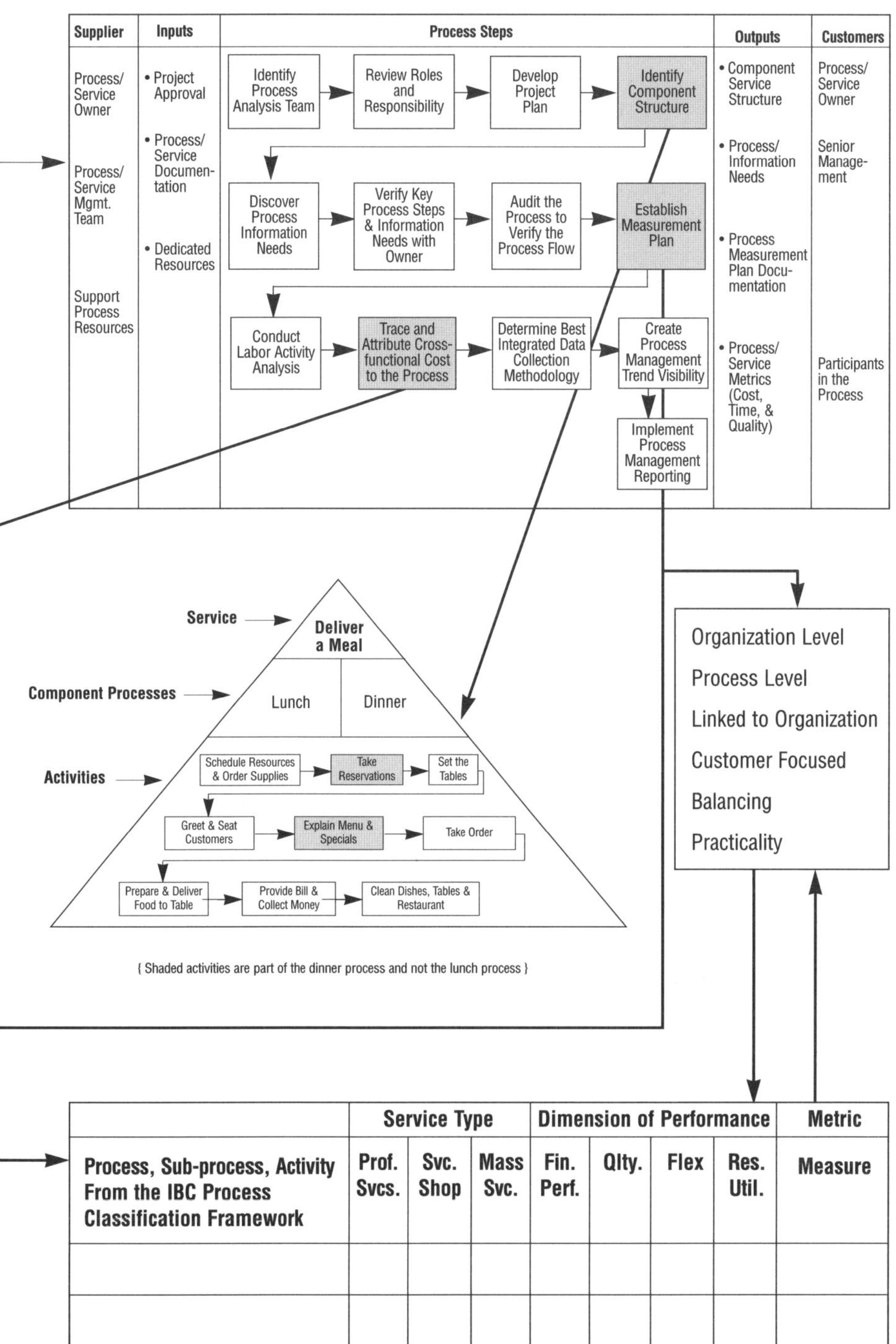
Supplier
Inputs
Process Steps
Outputs
Customers
Process/ Service Owner
Process/ Service Mgmt. Team
Support Process Resources
• Project Approval
• Process/ Service Documentation
• Dedicated Resources
Identify Process Analysis Team
Review Roles and Responsibility
Develop Project Plan
Identify Component Structure
Discover Process Information Needs
Verify Key Process Steps & Information Needs with Owner
Audit the Process to Verify the Process Flow
Establish Measurement Plan
Conduct Labor Activity Analysis
Trace and Attribute Cross-functional Cost to the Process
Determine Best Integrated Data Collection Methodology
Create Process Management Trend Visibility
Implement Process Management Reporting
• Component Service Structure
• Process/ Information Needs
• Process Measurement Plan Documentation
• Process/ Service Metrics (Cost, Time, & Quality)
Process/ Service Owner
Senior Management
Participants in the Process
Service
Deliver a Meal
Component Processes
Lunch
Dinner
Activities
Schedule Resources & Order Supplies
Take Reservations
Set the Tables
Greet & Seat Customers
Explain Menu & Specials
Take Order
Prepare & Deliver Food to Table
Provide Bill & Collect Money
Clean Dishes, Tables & Restaurant
{ Shaded activities are part of the dinner process and not the lunch process }
Organization Level
Process Level
Linked to Organization
Customer Focused
Balancing
Practicality
Service Type
Dimension of Performance
Metric
Process, Sub-process, Activity From the IBC Process Classification Framework
Prof. Svcs.
Svc. Shop
Mass Svc.
Fin. Perf.
Qlty.
Flex
Res. Util.
Measure

OTHER PUBLICATIONS AVAILABLE FROM THE CAM-I LIBRARY

CAPACITY MEASUREMENT & IMPROVEMENT A MANAGER'S GUIDE TO EVALUATING & OPTIMIZING CAPACITY PRODUCTIVITY

Authors: CAM-I Capacity Model Interest Group

In a competitive economy, the effective use of capacity is critical. Unfortunately, there has been no universal approach to measuring the effectiveness of capacity use. The model explained in this book provides this missing tool. The model helps evaluate and change how companies use and plan capacity.

Capacity Measurement & Improvement shows how capacity measurement can be used to provide strategic information that can help managers improve the productivity of existing capacity and facilitate intelligent capital investment decisions. Developed by the Capacity Model Interest Group of the CAM-I CMS Program, this book is a practical, reasoned approach to this critical manufacturing issue.

This book presents:

- A unique capacity model, researched and developed by CAM-I;
- Templates for application;
- Implementation procedures;
- Straightforward definitions, key point summaries; and illustrations to facilitate reader understanding.

Price – $35.

TARGET COSTING: THE NEXT FRONTIER IN STRATEGIC COST MANAGEMENT – A CAM-I / CMS MODEL FOR PROFIT PLANNING AND COST MANAGEMENT

Authors: CAM-I Target Cost Core Group & Profs. Ansari & Bell

This book provides practical insights on how to use target costing for profit planning and cost management. Target costing is strategic in nature and, if done properly, it creates a culture of excellence in an organization that provides continuing strategic advantage.

The authors relied on state-of-the-art practices drawn from translations of papers available only in the Japanese language and the collective experience of several world class companies, including: Arthur Andersen, The Boeing Company, Chrysler Corporation, Eastman Kodak Company and Texas Instruments.

Key topics include:

- How target costing relates to business strategy and profit planning;
- A process model that links target costing with the product development cycle;
- The linkages between customer requirements and costing;
- Tools, information systems and measurement systems required to support target costing.

Price – $50.

ABC MANAGER'S PRIMER

Authors: Gary Cokins, Alan Stratton and Jack Helbling

This document, written with a clear, informed understanding of what ABC is all about, is based on real implementation experiences. The "Three R's" now revitalizing the way business is conducted in the United States are Reengineering, Reinventing, and Redesigning processes. Traditionally, accounting systems are not designed to deliver managerial information. Activity-Based information significantly boosts the value and utility of financial data for decision makers and empowered employees. This primer addresses the lack of awareness of what ABC is and is not. It is not written as a "how-to-implement" cookbook, but does give a head start for action.

This is perhaps the world's most popular introduction to ABC concepts with over 30,000 copies sold.

Price – $15.

THE 60 MINUTE ABC BOOK FOR OPERATIONS MANAGEMENT

Author: Timothy White

This short-read manual presents the ABC concept in a simplified and straightforward manner, specifically for the understanding of non-financial management, and demonstrates that the "activity management" possibilities of ABC clearly distinguish it as an Operations Management tool.

Subjects discussed include:

- Traditional overhead costing methodology, basic ABC terminology, implementation and software considerations, and successful CAM-I member ABC implementation efforts.
- The manual includes an ABC tutorial diskette developed by Storage Technology Corporation which provides an in-depth description and analysis of the ABC methodology for those individuals desiring a more detailed knowledge of ABC than the 60 Minute Book provides.

Price – $20

THE ROAD TO EXCELLENCE BECOMING A PROCESS-BASED COMPANY

Revised and Edited by:
Dennis C. Daly
and Tom Freeman

The primary objective of this guide is to inform and educate companies about process-based management. It is a real world consolidation of process-based management experiences and provides an educational vehicle for management and workers to foster a better understanding of process-based management. The success and the survival of an organization depend on how well the organization manages its processes.

Successful management initiatives must be developed and framed within the context of a larger system. In order to achieve this objective it is necessary to take a "management systems" approach. The term "management system" involves all aspects of management including corporate strategy, information technology, leadership, organization structure, management processes and culture.

Learn which strategies drive processes and govern both the planning and learning phases of process management that will put you on The Road to Excellence.

Price – $30.

Consortium for Advanced Manufacturing-International

Bedford, Texas

The Consortium for Advanced Manufacturing-International (CAM-I) Cost Management Systems (CMS) Program is internationally recognized as the leading forum for the advancement of cost and resource management practices. Organized in 1986 as a coalition of leading thinkers from industry, government and academia, the CMS Program has accomplished extensive research and development of new management methods. The CMS Program is acknowledged world-wide for its development of Activity Based Costing (ABC) and Activity Based Management (ABM).

For information about other CAM-I publications,
or to receive a copy of the most current
CAM-I Library Catalog contact:

CAM-I Library Services
3301 Airport Freeway, Suite 324
Bedford, Texas 76021

Telephone 817/860-1654
FAX 817/275-6450

E-mail: nancyt@cam-i.org
http://www.cam-i.org/library.html